Family History for Kids

Family History for Kids

by Emma Jolly

PYMER QUANTRILL PUBLISHING

Published by
Pymer Quantrill Publishing Ltd
Registered number 06421679
www.pqpublishing.com
info@pqpublishing.com

First edition published December 2007

A catalogue record for this book is available from the British Library.

ISBN 978-0-9557578-0-8

Family History for Kids
Text: Emma Jolly
Editor: David Popey
Design: Pymer Quantrill Publishing
Illustration: Antony Cummins
www.acmed-art.co.uk

Printed in the UK by MRT Response Ltd

Contents

Welcome to Your Family History

Congratulations! You are about to embark on a fascinating journey into the past.

Family history is for everyone and about everyone. It is the history of families, and individuals; of places near and far away; of relaxation and very hard work; of poverty and riches; of friends and enemies; of fun and misery; of war and of peace.

This book is an introduction to the subject of family history (or **GENEALOGY**). To find out everything about your family's past can take forever. You may never find all the people you are descended from, and many family stories will remain undiscovered. But, by following the steps described in the following pages, you will begin to know more about your ancestors and how to research them. There is even a family tree on **pages 16 and 17** for you to fill in.

There are many ways in which you can use this book. **Pages 8-17** show you how to make the most of the resources you have around you, not least the family you live with. **Pages 18-29** show you how social and local history can help you discover more about your ancestors' everyday lives. **Pages 30-37** take family history into the history and events of a wider world. From this you can learn how your ancestors have been a part of major events in world history. **Pages 38-49** give you suggestions for doing family history, and provide an introduction to the methods and skills needed.

At the back of this book, you will find a glossary explaining the **KEYWORDS** highlighted throughout, as well as a detailed index. There are also some useful website addresses for further information.

Using this book

Family History for Kids **is full of helpful features:**

Keywords

Throughout the book you will see highlighted words and phrases e.g. **WORLD WAR TWO** Explanations of these keywords can be found in the glossary on pages 50-55.

National Curriculum

These symbols show where the content of the page may be relevant to the Key Stage you are studying at school. See page 60 for further details.

2

3

Information Boxes

Purple boxes give you more information about the background to a specific subject. Red boxes suggest further activities to try.

Project Sheets

These symbols show where a topic is covered further by one of the seven project sheets on pages 43-49.

PS1

PS7

The themes covered in this book provide the first steps for you to find out about your ancestors. After working through the activities, you may be inspired to find out more about a specific aspect of your family, or you may use it to add more detail to a school project. Several resources are listed on **pages 56-59** to make your research easier.

Finally, one of the reasons that family history is so interesting is that anyone can do it. It doesn't matter if you are adopted, or you don't know both of your biological parents. You can fill in the details of the family you live with, or the family you know about. There is so much to explore in your family's history that you should never be short of ideas about what to research next.

I hope you enjoy reading this book and taking your first steps in the world of family history.

Emma Jolly

My Family Name

A good starting point is the origin of your own surname. Last names may contain clues that could help trace your family as far back as the Middle Ages.

Where do I start?

Last names are an important starting point in helping you to complete your **FAMILY TREE** (see pages 16-17). If you have a surname that many other people share, such as JONES, SMITH or WILLIAMS, you may find it easier to begin your search with another family name. Try using the last name of a step parent or grandparent, or your mother's **MAIDEN NAME**. Common surnames will require much patience in your research – you may find it difficult to distinguish between different families as you go further back in history.

History of Surnames

We take it for granted that our last name comes from our parents as they inherited it from their own parents. It might seem strange but in the past, handwritten records show that the spelling of surnames changed quite frequently. This was because many people could not read or write.

A good example of this is William Shakespeare whose name was spelt variously as SHAKESPERE, SHAKESPEAR, SHAKSPERE and even SHEXPERE.

In fact, it was not until the mid-nineteenth century, when general education was introduced for everyone, that such differences began to disappear. People tended to use consistent spelling for their surnames. This means that you might expect to see different spellings of last names in your family records before the nineteenth century.

Even today people sometimes change their names. Immigrants may need to give themselves a new surname if they come from a country that does not use fixed last names. Some names are changed for professional reasons (e.g. an actor's stagename) or to avoid embarrassment.

Surnames in other cultures work according to different rules. In Spain, they come from the family names of both parents (originally from the father of each parent). In China, the name comes from the mother, while Pakistani surnames usually originate from tribal or ancestral names.

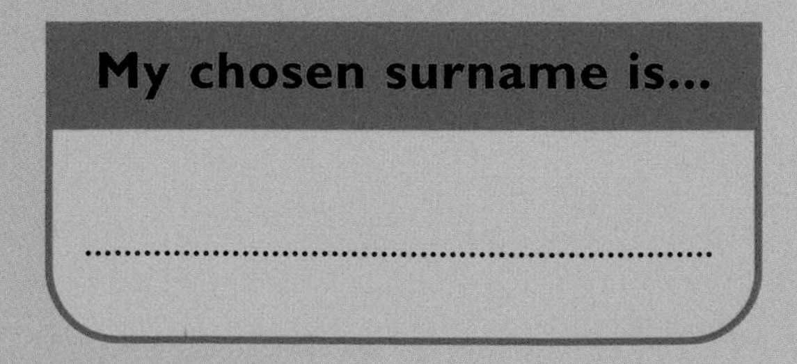

Origins of your Surname

There are four main origins of surnames in the UK:

Father to Son: A last name originally formed from a father's name is called a **PATRONYMIC**. Names such as Harrison literally once meant 'son of Harry'. There are many variations: the son of a man called David could be Mr DAVIDSON (David's son), DAVIES, DAVEY or DAVISON.

Location: Named after an actual place (e.g. ASHLEY a town in Wiltshire) or a description of an area (e.g. HILL, WOOD, MUIR (a moor), CRAIG (near a cliff or crag).

Occupation: Jobs also determined our ancestors' surnames. For example, FLETCHER (from the **OLD FRENCH** word *flechier*) meant "arrow-maker/arrow-seller". Weaver, Tailor, Draper and Cooper are all names that once indicated an occupation.

Nicknames: Some names may have developed from an ancestor's personality or appearance, e.g. JOLLY (a very happy person), KING (someone who played a lead role), REID (a Scottish name for someone with red hair).

Original surnames

You can find the original surname of your ancestor by looking at their birth certificate, marriage certificate or baptism records. It was usual for a woman in England and Wales to take her husband's name when she married, so be prepared for names in later documents to be different from the birth certificate. In some cases men may also change their surname.

Activities

- Make a list of surnames in your family. Which one is the rarest name?
- Make a list of surnames of other people you know. How many are named after nearby places? How easily can you find out about the origin of their names?
- Find a surname dictionary in your local library. What can it tell you about your last name?

- See page 64 for an example surname analysis.

Interviewing My Family

Talking to members of your family is a great way to find out more about your ancestors. The tips on this page will help you become a family historian almost immediately!

Ask your parents or guardian about other members of the family and how they are related to you. It always helps to keep a note of first names and surnames. Parents, Aunts, Uncles, Grandparents and Cousins will all be able to tell you something you did not know about your ancestors.

Contacting People

Keep in mind that it might be difficult to contact members of your family. They may no longer keep in touch or they may live far away. There are many ways you can contact them. Write a letter to introduce yourself if you have never met before. Your relative may prefer to write back and provide family details.

If they have an e-mail address, this may be a quick way to contact them. Calling by telephone is also an option, but always ask for permission from whoever pays the bill – the relative may live in another country and the call could be expensive.

Always respect other people's wishes if they do not want to talk. Some people like to keep their family's history private.

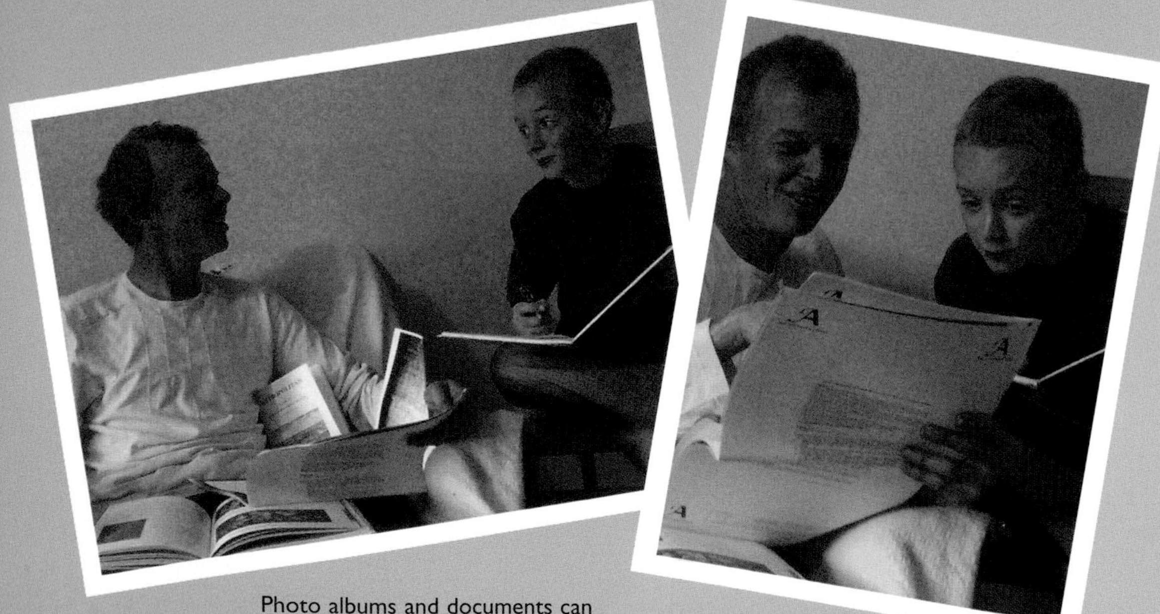

Photo albums and documents can help prompt memories about the past.

Getting Ready

When preparing for an interview, it's always useful to have the following items with you:

- Pen/pencil and notepad
- Cassette or digital recorder
- Spare batteries
- Camera

Always ask before recording an interview. Some people prefer not to be recorded and they concentrate better if they do not feel self-conscious. You may also want to take a photo. Always ask permission first.

Visit with biscuits or a favourite snack – this may help your relative relax.

Asking Questions

When you speak to family members, begin with simple questions like, "What is your full name?" This will help you complete the family tree on pages 16 and 17. Most importantly, let your relative speak – don't interrupt!

Generating Memories

Try specific questions that might help evoke memories. For example:

- "What did you eat for breakfast when you were growing up?"
- "How did you celebrate your birthday?"
- "What clothes did you wear in winter?"
- "Who was your best friend?"

Objects and Photographs

Before the interview starts, ask to see any old photographs that your relative has in their home. A photo album often shows family events and celebrations, and how your ancestors lived and worked. If you have already interviewed other members of your family, why not bring along an item they have provided. This could be a photo or an object that will help your relative remember stories and information about their past.

Find out more

Family photographs......pages 12-13
Family documents.........pages 14-15

Always treat other people's possessions with care and ask before you touch any items. Most objects they show you will be very old and could be fragile.

Sometimes family documents or medals were passed down to one member of the family. This may have been the eldest child, or perhaps the last child to have remained unmarried. As such, your parents or grandparents may not be the guardians of the family papers. Ask your parents if they know who else may have useful documents.

Looking at My Family Photographs

Family photos can provide vital clues about events such as weddings or birthdays. Show them to other family members and write down any information they can provide. See how much you can find out.

Asking Questions about a Photograph

Who?

- Who are the people in the photograph? What are they doing?
- How are you related to them?

What?

- What's the occasion?
- What religion is this family?
- What clues tell you this?

Where?

- Where was the photo taken? Look for clues such as the background, the people in the photograph and the occasion. It might not always be obvious from the photo.

When?

- What time of year is it? Look at the weather, the leaves and plants, and the type of clothes.
- What year is it? There could be a date on the back of the photo. This picture was taken in 1931.

Looking Closer

Ask yourself as many questions as possible about the photos you find and pay careful attention to what your relatives tell you. You will be surprised what you can learn with a little extra research.

Hats

Most of the women are wearing cloche-style hats. These were popular in the 1920s and 1930s. A cloche hat is named after the French word for bell, as it is shaped like one. It fits closely around the head. Most women here are wearing a version of the hat with a longer brim.

Collars

The formal collar shown here was often worn for ocassions such as weddings. Notice, it is the younger men in the photograph that tend to be wearing these kind of collars.

Hairstyles

The bridesmaids at the front of the photo have short hair waved in curls and parted on the side. In the 1920s, the fashion tended to straight hair, so this photo may have been taken in the 1930s.

What next?

- Describe a wedding you've been to. In what ways was it similar to the wedding seen here? How was it different?
- Look at photos in your family album. What can they tell you about how your family lived?
- Keep a note of everything your relatives can tell you about pictures that belong to your family.

My Family Documents

You will find many different documents when you study your family's history.

Talk to your relatives and ask them to show you any family documents they may have. These could include:

- Birth, Marriage or Death (**BMD**) Certificates
- School Certificates
- Newspapers containing funeral notices or articles about the family
- Certificates from work
- Papers from the Army, Navy or Air Force
- Medals
- Letters
- Inscribed watches
- Books with notes or messages (such as a Family Bible, passed down through generations).

Certificates

Most people in England and Wales should have registered the **Births** of their children, their **Marriages** and **Deaths** in the family.

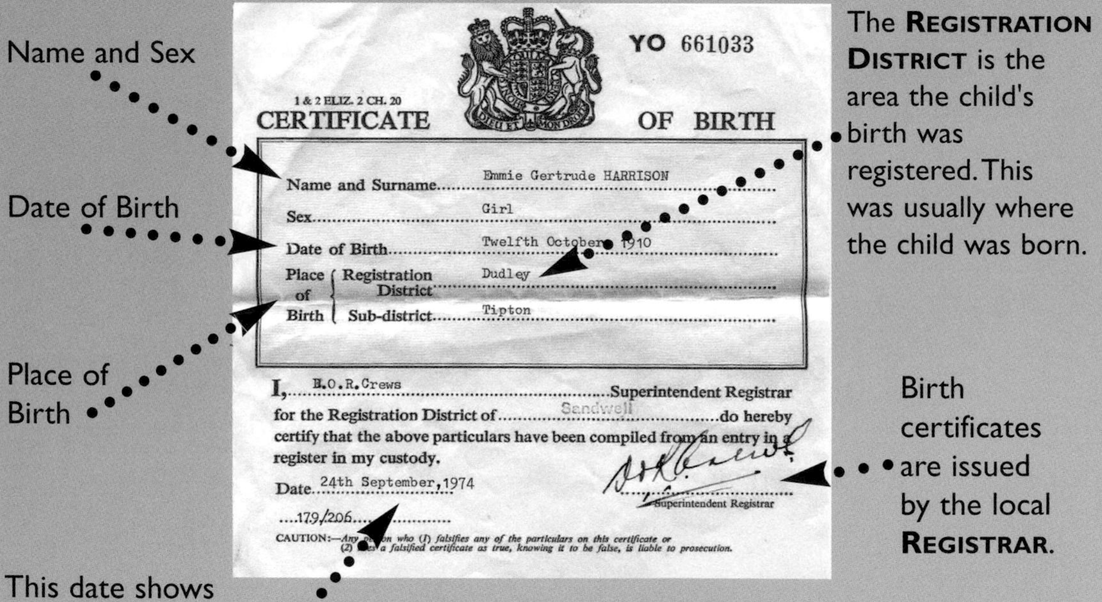

YO 661033

1 & 2 ELIZ. 2 CH. 20

CERTIFICATE OF BIRTH

Name and Surname: Emmie Gertrude HARRISON
Sex: Girl
Date of Birth: Twelfth October 1910
Place of Birth – Registration District: Dudley
Place of Birth – Sub-district: Tipton

I, H.O.R. Crews, Superintendent Registrar for the Registration District of Sandwell do hereby certify that the above particulars have been compiled from an entry in a register in my custody.

Date 24th September, 1974

Superintendent Registrar

179/206

CAUTION:—Any person who (1) falsifies any of the particulars on this certificate or (2) uses a falsified certificate as true, knowing it to be false, is liable to prosecution.

This date shows when this copy of the certificate was issued.
Be careful! This is not the same as the date of the birth (or the date of registration).

This is a short birth certificate. A full version will give you more details: the exact place of birth, the name (including **maiden name**) and residence of the mother, and the name and occupation of the father. Some certificates will give the occupation of the mother. This can help you to trace your family back another **generation**.

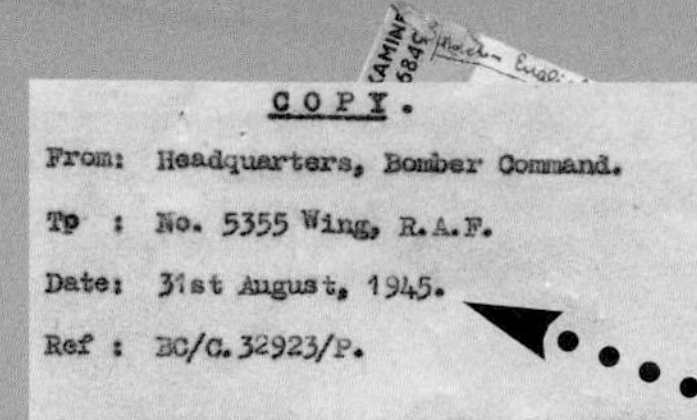

COPY.

From: Headquarters, Bomber Command.

To : No. 5355 Wing, R.A.F.

Date: 31st August, 1945.

Ref : BC/G.32923/P.

PUBLICITY CAMPAIGN TO ENCOURAGE APPLICATIONS FROM AIRMEN TO REMAIN IN THE ROYAL AIR FORCE ON A REGULAR ENGAGEMENT.

With reference to your letter, 5355W/1226/P3 dated 19th August, 1945., which forwarded a proposal from 991536 F/Sgt. Jolly, O.D., to encourage applications from airmen to remain in the Royal Air Force on a regular engagement, you are requested to inform this airman that his proposal has been forwarded to Air Ministry for such action as that department consider necessary.

2. The interest shown by F/Sgt. Jolly in the recruiting campaign for the regular Air Force is greatly appreciated and he should be brought before his Commanding Officer and commended for his practical suggestion.

(Signed) ?????? G/Capt.,
Air Vice Marshall,
i/c Administration,
BOMBER COMMAND.

Letters and Military Documents

You may find correspondence that gives clues to an ancestor's job, or military activity.

Make a note of the date. We can see that Flight Sergeant Jolly was in the **RAF** in August 1945.

Make a note of any military numbers. These numbers may help to identify the same person in other records.

Always note the address at the top of the page, and the name at the bottom. These show who sent the letter.

Name of the church (the local **ARCHIVE** should have more details)

Religious Documents

Documents such as Baptism Records provide many clues.

Type of religion (here, it is Christian)

Person's name

Date of the ceremony

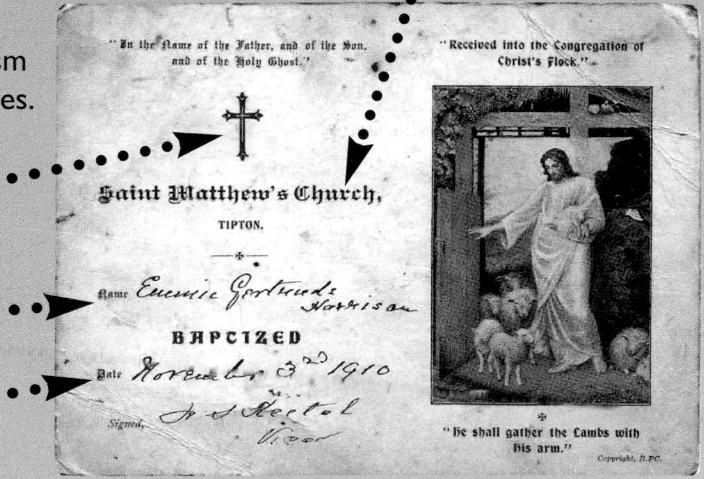

Using the Census

The **CENSUS** is a complete record of every household in the country. It is used by the government to collect statistics about the population.

In the UK, the census is taken every 10 years. It is an invaluable tool for family historians even though recent records are not yet accessible by the public (the 1901 census is the latest available).

You can use censuses to discover where your ancestors were living, who they lived with, their age, and the jobs they did. It is a good way to track your family over time. Later censuses have a birthplace column which helps find out where your ancestors came from. Most family historians use online indexes to find their ancestors in the censuses (**see pages 58-59**).

My Family Tree

How to use

Start by filling in your own details in the largest box and add a recent photo of yourself. Then, work across the page entering as many details as possible about your ancestors (use the example, right, as a guide). Ask a family member to help you with details you are unsure about.

Sample entry

Grandfather

Name..... *Thomas*......
J. Mann..Born.*1920*.
at......*Norwich*............
Job.....*Engineer*.........
Married Died
..*1946*.... ..*1999*....

Me

Name....................................

Born....................................

at...

My Brothers and Sisters

....

....

....

Put your photo here

Mother

Name...............................
Born................................
at.....................................
Married...........................
Job...................................

=

Father

Name...............................
Born................................
at.....................................
Married...........................
Job...................................

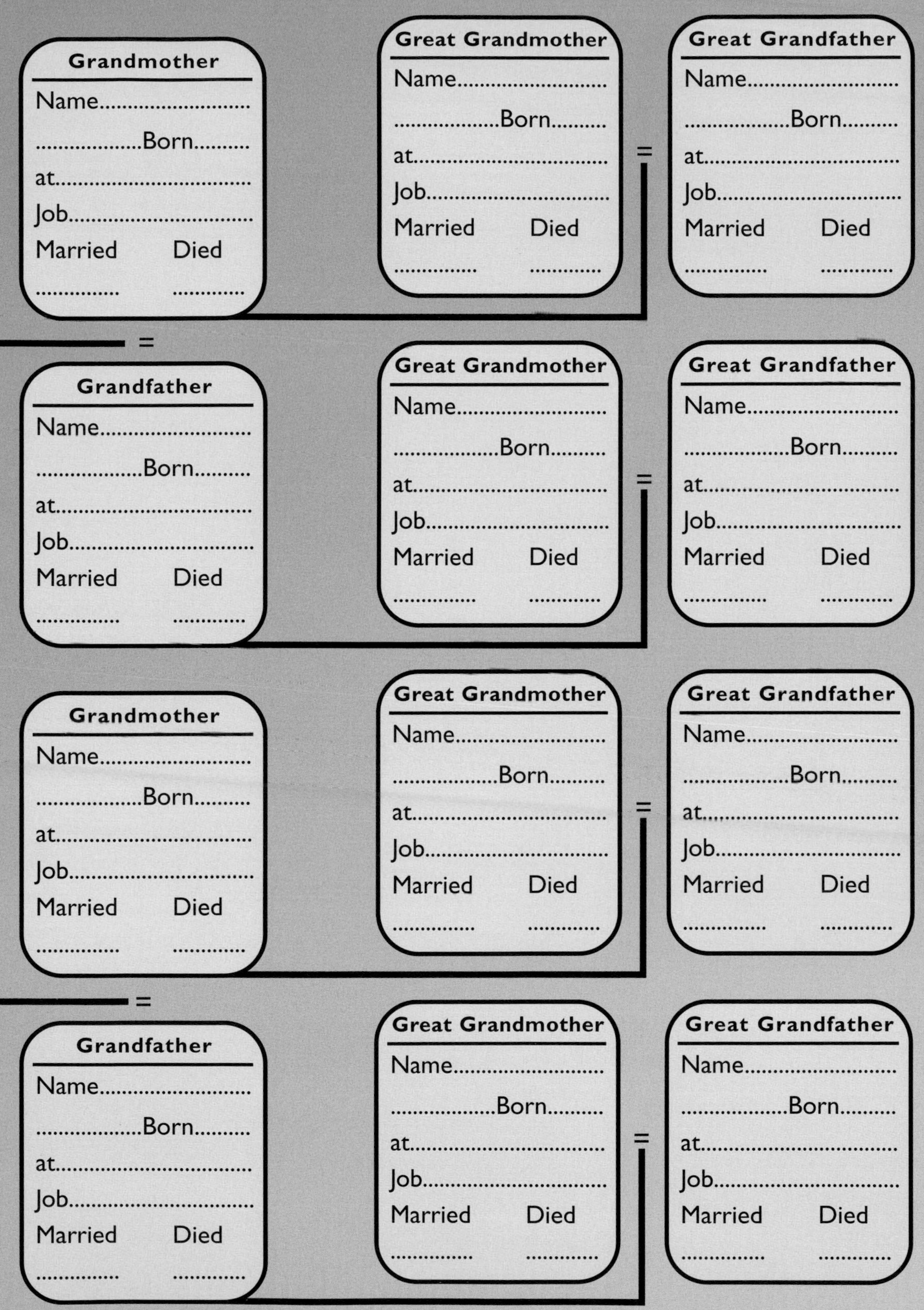

Grandmother
Name..........................
..................Born..........
at..................................
Job................................
Married Died
....

Great Grandmother
Name..........................
..................Born..........
at..................................
Job................................
Married Died
....

=

Great Grandfather
Name..........................
..................Born..........
at..................................
Job................................
Married Died
....

=

Grandfather
Name..........................
..................Born..........
at..................................
Job................................
Married Died
....

Great Grandmother
Name..........................
..................Born..........
at..................................
Job................................
Married Died
....

=

Great Grandfather
Name..........................
..................Born..........
at..................................
Job................................
Married Died
....

Grandmother
Name..........................
..................Born..........
at..................................
Job................................
Married Died
....

Great Grandmother
Name..........................
..................Born..........
at..................................
Job................................
Married Died
....

=

Great Grandfather
Name..........................
..................Born..........
at..................................
Job................................
Married Died
....

=

Grandfather
Name..........................
..................Born..........
at..................................
Job................................
Married Died
....

Great Grandmother
Name..........................
..................Born..........
at..................................
Job................................
Married Died
....

=

Great Grandfather
Name..........................
..................Born..........
at..................................
Job................................
Married Died
....

2 3 PS6 PS7

MY FAMILY TIMELINE

The lives of our ancestors are linked very closely with the events of local, national and international history. Wars, taxes and laws have all had major effects on our families. You may have an ancestor or relation who was involved in a war.

	18th Century	19th Century
Kings and Queens	William III 1689-1702 Anne 1702-1714 George I 1714-1727 George II 1727-1760	George III 1760-1820 George IV 1820-1830 William IV 1830-1837 Victoria 1837-1901
Events	**1707:** **ACT OF UNION** created the Kingdom of Great Britain **1721:** the first British Prime Minister, Sir Robert Walpole **1752:** the **GREGORIAN CALENDAR** starts **1750s:** **AGRICULTURAL REVOLUTION** begins **1760s:** **INDUSTRIAL REVOLUTION** begins with James Watt's steam engine **1775-83:** American War of Independence **1776:** Declaration of American Independence from Britain. **1787:** **TRANSPORTATION** of convicts to Australia begins **1789:** French Revolution **1793-1815:** Revolutionary & Napoleonic Wars (including Battle of Trafalgar in 1805)	**1800s:** Industrial Revolution continues **1807:** Abolition of British **SLAVE** Trade **1825:** First steam locomotive to carry passengers **1829:** The Metropolitan Police is founded **1835:** Photography is invented **1837:** Civil registration of births, marriages and deaths (**BMD**) begins in England and Wales **1841:** National Census (the first useful **CENSUS** for family historians (see pages 15 and 50) **1845-51:** Irish potato famine **1876:** Invention of the telephone **1881:** Eastern European **POGROMS** begin – many Jews settle in England **1899-1902:** Boer Wars

My Family

My family in the 18th and 19th centuries:

....

....

....

....

....

....

....

....

Your family may have moved from another area of the UK to find work. Perhaps they migrated from a different country to escape persecution or an unfair law? **See pages 30-35** for information about ancestors from across the world.

20th Century

Edward VII 1901-1910
George V 1910-1936
Edward VIII 1936
George VI 1936-1952 Elizabeth II 1952-

- **1900s:** Beginnings of Radio
- **1914-18:** First World War
- **1922: Partition** of Ireland
- **1926:** Television invented
- **1927:** Adopted Children's Register created (see page 50)
- **1928:** All women gain the right to vote
- **1929: Wall Street Crash** and the beginnings of the **Depression**
- **1939-45:** Second World War
- **1945-90s: Cold War**
- **1947:** India gains **INDEPENDENCE**
- **1948:** NHS established in the UK
- **1948:** Post-war migration begins with arrival of the **Empire Windrush** (p32-33)
- **1970s:** Beginnings of the Internet
- **1973:** Britain joins the **EEC** (now **EU**)
- **1979:** Margaret Thatcher becomes the first female British Prime Minister
- **1982:** Falklands War
- **1989:** Fall of the Berlin Wall
- **1990-1:** 1st Gulf War

21st Century

- **2000:** Millennium celebrations
- **2001:** Terrorist attacks on New York
- **2003:** Mapping of Human Genome completed
- **2003:** Second Gulf War

My family in the 20th and 21st centuries:

2 3 PS3 PS6

WHERE DID MY FAMILY WORK?

There are many ways to find out what members of your family once did for a living. Start by asking your parents about the jobs they have done in the past. How do they compare with what they do now?

The types of jobs we do have changed enormously in the past two hundred years. In the centuries preceding the **INDUSTRIAL REVOLUTION**, most of the population (more than 85%) worked on the land.

Today, many people in the UK work in offices and use computers. Less than 1.5% of the population earn their living from working in agriculture.

Being a job detective

How can I find out what my ancestors did for a living?

- Ask your family and relatives about their working lives and the jobs that their parents did.
- Look at birth, marriage and death certificates (**BMD**). These should always list the occupation of the parents or person named on the form or list.
- Find **PARISH REGISTERS** and **CENSUS** information. Military records from the **FIRST** and **SECOND WORLD WARS** will also include your ancestor's **CIVILIAN** occupation.

Why did Great Grandma not have a job?

Your Great Grandma probably did work, but often women's occupations were not listed on records such as marriage certificates, for example. Therefore, it can appear that your female ancestors didn't have a job.

Often women stopped working when they married or became pregnant, but they may have worked for years previously. Many children and teenagers (including women) worked full-time in the past, in jobs such as labourering, brick-making, or spinning cotton in factories. Between having children or when their kids were older, women may have returned to a job they could do at home. Some women are listed on the **CENSUS** as laundress, nurse, housemaid, cook; or working at home in a trade such as **STRAW PLAITING** or **SPINNING**.

Find out...

Where have the women in your family worked?

MOTHER.................................

....

GRANDMOTHER.....................

....

....

Job Descriptions

Your ancestors may have had one of the jobs described below.

- Try to imagine what life would have been like working in these jobs.
- How many hours did they work?
- How much money did they earn?

Agricultural Labourer

Most ancestors living in Britain up to the early 1800s worked on the land. Some were farmers (owning or managing a farm), but most were agricultural labourers. Work was varied and very hard. The hours were long and the pay was not good. From the 1870s, fewer workers were needed and many labourers left the countryside to find work in the factories and new industries of the growing towns and cities.

A group of servants in the 1860s

Domestic Servant

Domestic service was a very popular type of job for women in the late 19th and early 20th centuries. As a domestic servant, a girl could learn how to run a house. She was given lodging and food, which enabled her to work away from home. This required many women to move some distance from their home. Men worked as servants too, and women often met a future husband at work. Whereas women were usually cooks, nurses, or housemaids, men worked as grooms, butlers, kitchen hands, or gardeners.

Most farm workers worked long hours and were very poorly paid.

Railway Worker

The railway was a new form of transport in the nineteenth century. Emerging industries liked using trains to send their goods around Britain because they were quicker than canal boats and horse-drawn coaches. Workers were needed to lay the tracks, build the engines and run the trains. The first trains were powered by steam, and workers became very dirty from all the soot and smoke.

Lawyer

Lawyers give advice to people about the law. They may be judges, advocates, attorneys, barristers, QCs or solicitors. Working in law was once a profession open to only the middle and upper classes.

To find out if any of your ancestors was a judge, magistrate or solicitor look at the following records:

- For lawyers since 1780, check the **LAW LIST**
- Judges: try a **BIOGRAPHICAL DICTIONARY** from your local library.
- Records of students at the **INNS OF COURT** and **INNS OF CHANCERY** are often held at your main library.

Quiz: Jobs from the Past

All of these phrases describe real jobs from the past. Can you work out what they did?

ALE DRAPER

....

ANKLE BEATER

....

CLAY PUDDLER

....

CROFTER

....

CUTLER

....

FELMONGER

....

HABERDASHER

....

KNACKER

....

OSTLER

....

RAG & BONE MAN

....

REEVE

....

TALLOW CHANDLER

....

VICTUALLER

....

YEOMAN

....

Are there any modern day equivalents to these jobs?

Answers are listed on page 64.

Find out more...

The following resources will help you find out more about your ancestors' jobs. Ask an adult to help you find them in your local library or local studies centre.

- Trade Directories include lists of old trades, and the people who did a certain type of job.
- Post Office Directories include lists of streets: if you know where your ancestor lived, check the entry for the street to see if his or her job is listed.
- The National Register of Archives (see **TNA** website) holds lists of Business Records. If your ancestor worked for a large company it is worth checking if it is listed here.
- Did your ancestor train as an apprentice? Your county record office or the Guildhall in London may hold records on their early career.
- Refer to the *Dictionary of Old Trades, Titles & Occupations* (by Colin Waters).

Social Class and My Family

Class generally refers to the way different groups of people are divided according to income, wealth, job and education. Knowing about an ancestor's class can help you understand how he/she may have lived.

Most of us are descended from working-class ancestors. In the 1901 census, more than three-quarters of people were described in this way. At the time, the term included craftsmen, merchants, traders and labourers (generally people who worked with their hands). A small, but significant, proportion of people were from the middle classes which included managers and Professionals – mainly those who worked in the Church, the Law, or Medicine. Later this class also included businessmen, shopkeepers, clerks, managers (banks), civil servants and teachers. The upper classes were generally made up of the aristocracy and **LANDED GENTRY**. However, this changed over time as the aristocracy began to lose their money, and industrialists and politicians began to gain more wealth and influence over the nation.

Those in the upper classes are generally considered to be the most powerful people in society. They usually had more wealth and property, a better education, a more comfortable occupation, and they could often make decisions which affected the lives of lower class people.

However, the definitions of the different classes have changed much in the last two hundred years. The previously accepted divisions of working/lower class, middle class and upper class are no longer accurate.

Jobs and Class

What class did these workers fit into in the 1800s?

- Agricultural Labourer
- Member of the **House of Lords**
- Landowner
- Servant
- Surgeon

An ancestor's home can give clues about his/her class.

Today, people are more likely to be described in different ways – not just through how much property they own or how much they earn.

Class Mobility
In the late 19th century, the class structure began to alter and it became easier for people to move between classes. This ease of movement is known as **CLASS MOBILITY**.

For example, improvements in education made it easier for a working-class person to get a job that was previously only held by someone from the middle classes. Like many today, people in the past were often ambitious. Some of your ancestors may have wanted to earn more money than their parents. They may have wanted to live in a bigger house or give their children a better future.

People could also move downwards; an upper-class man could become working or middle class by losing his money or position in society.

Generally, people moved between classes in the following ways:

- **Education** – which led to better employment prospects
- **Investment** – buying land or putting money into property
- **Marriage** – marrying a person with more money
- **Migration** – moving to an area where they could have a better standard of living.

Servants
Once, it was not unusual for richer people to have others to serve them. The phrase 'Upstairs/ Downstairs' describes the divide between employers and their staff. The servants of upper or middle class people tended to live and work in the basement or ground floor of a house. This was the 'downstairs' whilst the family of the house lived 'upstairs'.

Why does class matter?
Class is important to your family's history because it can help you understand how your ancestors thought about such issues as work and money. Many people felt restricted by their social class. They believed that their job, the places they lived in and their futures were all defined by their class.

Find out more...

- Think about the class of your ancestors. What clues might you be able to find about their class?
- Look back to pages 12 and 13. How could photos help you?
- Try reading *A Little Princess* (1905) by Frances Hodgson Burnett. This novel is about a girl from a wealthy family who is forced to live life as a servant.

The Women in My Family

It can be difficult to find out details about your female ancestors. Understanding how women's roles have changed during the last century may help you discover more about them.

Childbirth and Children

In the past, childbirth could be very dangerous. Most women gave birth at home without a doctor present. There may have been midwives, but many women were supported by their mothers or other female relatives. If anything went wrong during or after the birth, there was little that could be done to help. As a result, many babies and women died.

Pregnant women and mothers were often **DISCRIMINATED** against. They could be prevented from working and told that 'a woman's place is in the home'.

Unmarried women who had children, met with strong disapproval from all areas of society (especially by parish and civil authorities who had to pay for a child which received no money from the father). A child born in this way was considered to be **ILLEGITIMATE**.

Marriage

Once she was married, a woman became the property of her husband. All money and land that she owned now belonged to her husband for him to do as he pleased. The husband also had the power to beat his wife, and have her committed to an **ASYLUM**.

Women and Work

A single woman often could not support herself very well without the help of a husband or father. Many manual jobs, skilled work, and careers were not open to women and very few earned much money.

Examples of jobs done by unmarried or widowed working-class women in the late nineteenth century:

- A maid, children's nurse or cook in someone else's home.
- Cotton Worker (**WEAVER**, **SPINNER**, **CARDER** etc.)
- Mill Hand (or other Mill Job)
- Industrial work
- Home-based work (e.g. Dressmaker, Laundress, Ironer).

Looking Back

Ask your mother, grandmothers and great-grandmothers about their lives:

- Did they all vote?
- At what ages did they marry?
- What clothes did they wear?
- What kind of education did they have?
- Do they think life is better or worse for girls today?

Fighting for Equality

In the late nineteenth and early twentieth century the **SUFFRAGISM** movement demanded that women also be given the right to vote. One of the most famous leaders of this cause, Emmeline Pankhurst, was imprisoned on several occasions after demonstrating for the right of women to vote in elections and have a say in public life. The **SUFFRAGETTES** moved to greater and greater extremes in their protest, smashing windows, chaining themselves to railings and resorting to hunger strikes to enforce their demands. After many years, the government finally allowed women over the age of 30 to vote and by the end of 1928, all women 21 and over were able to vote.

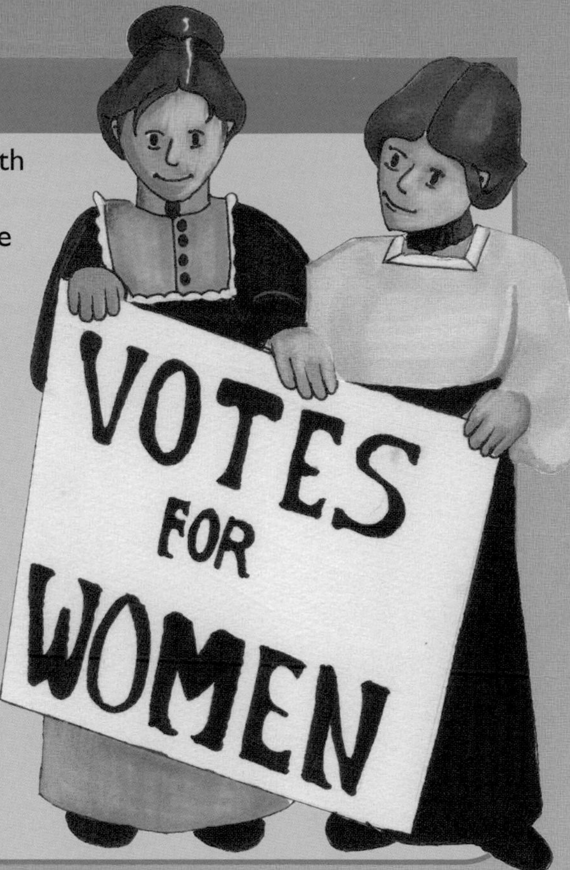

Helping at Home

If they had no job, working-class women usually helped their mothers or sisters at home or ran the house for their father. They may have taken in lodgers to help pay for the rent.

By contrast, women from wealthier backgrounds were often educated at home or at boarding school. However, they were expected to be wives and mothers above all else. Some middle-class women may have found work as a governess or a tutor but very few were allowed to have a professional career.

Much of this started to change when women pushed for equal rights with men in different areas of society (see box above).

War Work

The **FIRST WORLD WAR** opened up many working opportunities for women. Whilst men were away fighting, women were needed to work as nurses (at home and abroad), make **MUNITIONS** and keep public transport running. After the war, many women returned to being wives and mothers.

In the **SECOND WORLD WAR** women were required to do more varied and more demanding work. Some joined the Armed Forces and a few worked as spies and interpreters.

Find out more about...

Family Jobs........................pages 20-23
My Family in Wartime.....pages 36-37

WHAT DID MY FAMILY EAT?

Another way to understand how your ancestors lived is to find out about the food they ate. How has it changed from what you eat today? Some foods will be very familiar and others very different.

Local Food

In the past, food generally came from local sources – much more than it does today. When most of the population worked in agriculture, finding food in the countryside could be easier, especially at **HARVEST TIME**. However, many rural people went hungry. A crop failure could be disastrous for a local community who depended on it for their food. Most families were too poor to keep animals for food. Fruit and nuts from trees and hedgerows, and herbs could be plentiful but were not available all year round.

People who lived by the coast had access to fish and seafood. Sometimes fish like pilchards, anchovies, **HERRING** and **SALMON** were salted and smoked to preserve them for times when the fish were far away from the shore. Fish and chips have been popular in Britain since the 1860s when railways began transporting fish at speed to inner cities. Hungry industrial workers could then enjoy the food at a cheap price.

During the **INDUSTRIAL REVOLUTION**, many **URBAN** families lived on **CEREALS**, meat, potatoes, beer, sugar, and tea. However, most had no garden or access to fresh vegetables and were poorly nourished by cheap food bought with low wages. Some **INDUSTRIALISTS**, such as the Cadbury brothers in Birmingham, created housing for their workers that included gardens for them to grow food.

Rationing during the Second World War

Food was not always as readily available as it is today. In the 1930s, Britain imported over 50 million tons of food each year but during the Second World War food had to be rationed. Ships carrying food were attacked and sunk by **U-BOATS**. As a result of this, and the pressures of feeding troops fighting abroad, there was not enough food in Britain.

Garden owners were asked to **'DIG FOR VICTORY'** and grow fruit and vegetables at home. Everyone in Britain, from the King to the poorest people, were only allowed the same ration per day.

• see **page 37** for a list of daily rations.

Making Mrs Beeton's Jam

Isabella Mary Beeton (1836–1865), is one of the best known cookery writers in British history. Her book, *Mrs Beeton's Book of Household Management* (1861), was a popular collection of more than 900 recipes. They give a good idea of the kinds of foods our ancestors would have eaten. Ask an adult to help you make the recipe below (Note 1lb. = 453g).

Gooseberry Jam
INGREDIENTS – To each lb. of fruit allow 1 lb. of preserving sugar, and a half pint of cold water.

METHOD – Top and tail the gooseberries. Dissolve the sugar in the cold water, boil up, simmer for about 15 minutes, and remove the scum as it rises. Now put in the fruit, boil gently from 35 to 40 minutes, or until the jam sets readily when tested on a cold plate. Pour into pots, cover at once with paper brushed over on both sides with white of egg, and store in a cool, dry place.
TIME – About 1 and a half hours.

Eating Meat

In the UK, meat has always been an important part of what we eat.

However, in the past it was often a luxury. Poor families could not afford to waste any part of the animal. Items such as a pig's cheek, ears, trotters, kidneys and tongue were all put to use. Cheap sources of meat included tripe (a cow's stomach) which was also recommended for people recovering from an illness because it could be digested easily. Mutton (an older sheep) was very popular – especially in stews. From a lamb, people ate the head, tail and shoulder. Today, most supermarkets only sell lamb but people once had to eat what they could.

Rich ancestors enjoyed hunting animals such as deer or pheasants for fun, but also to provide food. Poorer ancestors may have risked severe punishment or **TRANSPORTATION** to Australia for **POACHING** or stealing **GAME** from the land of wealthier people.

Food lists

- Make a food and drink diary for a week. Where does your food come from? Was it grown in a garden or allotment? Was it from a shop – what kind?
- Ask your grandparents to tell you where their food came from. What shops did they use?
- Do any members of your family remember food rationing? Find out how they managed to have enough to eat.

2 3

ANCESTORS ACROSS THE WORLD

Do you have family members from other parts of the world? Perhaps one of your ancestors lived or worked abroad or migrated from another country? See what you can find out.

Finding out about ancestors who travelled or lived abroad can be difficult. However, when you start to learn about the places your family came from, your research will become much easier.

Remember – many records from archives abroad are available to access online (see pages 58-59).

The Age of Empires

The growth of the British Empire led to many Britons living overseas and many people from around the world settling in Britain. Wars were often connected to the activities of empires. Our ancestors may have lived abroad or moved to Britain as a result of what happened during a war. Perhaps you were born abroad?

Most empires began with trade. The British Empire grew out of exploration, trading and settlement in the sixteenth and seventeenth centuries. Many of the explorers and traders wanted to be rich. In this period, America (now the USA) was settled by Britons, eager to produce tobacco, cotton, and sugar cane – and sell it to merchants back home. However, following the **American War of Independence,** Britain needed to develop its interests elsewhere and trade was a driving factor.

Did you know?

In 2007, 7.5% of people living in the UK were born in another country. Many more people are either related or descended from migrants.

India and the British Empire

The Empire in India grew out of the **East India Company**. This began as a group of London businessmen importing spices from South Asia (or the East Indies). However competition amongst spice traders (especially from Dutch traders) became so fierce that the Company even developed its own army. From 1857, India was controlled exclusively by the **British Colonial Office**.

India and Trade

Many goods were exported from India to Britain. These included **jute**, spices, silk, and tea. But the most valuable export was cotton cloth. In the 19th century, the British cotton industry grew, and the Government set taxes that made importing cloth from India too costly. From then on mainly raw cotton was sent to Britain. This left many Indians without work and led to famine and economic problems.

India and Pakistan gained **INDEPENDENCE** from Britain in 1947. Many Indian and Pakistani people have migrated to Britain in the twentieth century and as a result, close links between Britain and the Indian sub-continent have continued. Many Indian, Pakistani and Banglasdeshi people have migrated to Britain for work and study.

Case Study 1: Uganda

Many Indian people also lived in other British **COLONIES** In East Africa such as Kenya and Uganda. During the 1960s political problems in those countries forced them to leave. Most had British passports and Britain had promised to look after all **EXPATRIATE** or **DIASPORA** Indians.

In 1971 the Uganda leader, Idi Amin, gave Asian people three months to leave the country. Most were very prosperous people, but they were forced to leave everything behind and set up a new life in Britain. Around 21,000 Ugandans were re-settled into life in West London, Leicester, Birmingham and parts of Yorkshire.

Nihal's story

Nihal was born in Leicester in 1997. His parents, Sunil and Nia, have lived there since 1971 when they arrived as children from Uganda. Sunil's family were wealthy when they lived in Uganda.

When they arrived in Britain, however, life was difficult. Sunil's father had help from other family members to set up a newsagent which he ran until he retired. Sunil now runs the shop and Nihal helps him in the school holidays. Nihal likes living in Leicester and has many friends.

Britain and Africa

Britain first became involved with African countries because they were on or near trade routes to India. Whenever tensions occurred in countries like Egypt, Britain took charge as a way of preventing their own trade from being harmed.

There have been Africans in Britain since the Roman period, and seamen from West Africa have visited and lived here since the sixteenth century. More recently, African people have moved to Britain to study.

In the 1950s and 60s most African countries (for example Sierra Leone, Somalia, Nigeria, Ghana, Kenya, Ethiopia and Eritrea) gained their independence, and became part of the **COMMONWEALTH OF NATIONS.**

Today, people from these countries migrate and seek **ASYLUM** in Britain to escape wars, oppression, and poverty.

As many of these nations were formerly parts or **PROTECTORATES** of the British Empire, the ancestors of today's immigrants saw themselves as British or part-British.

Migration Map

This map shows some of the major migrations to and from Britain covered on pages 30-35. Were your ancestors part of these movements of people? Do you know why they migrated?

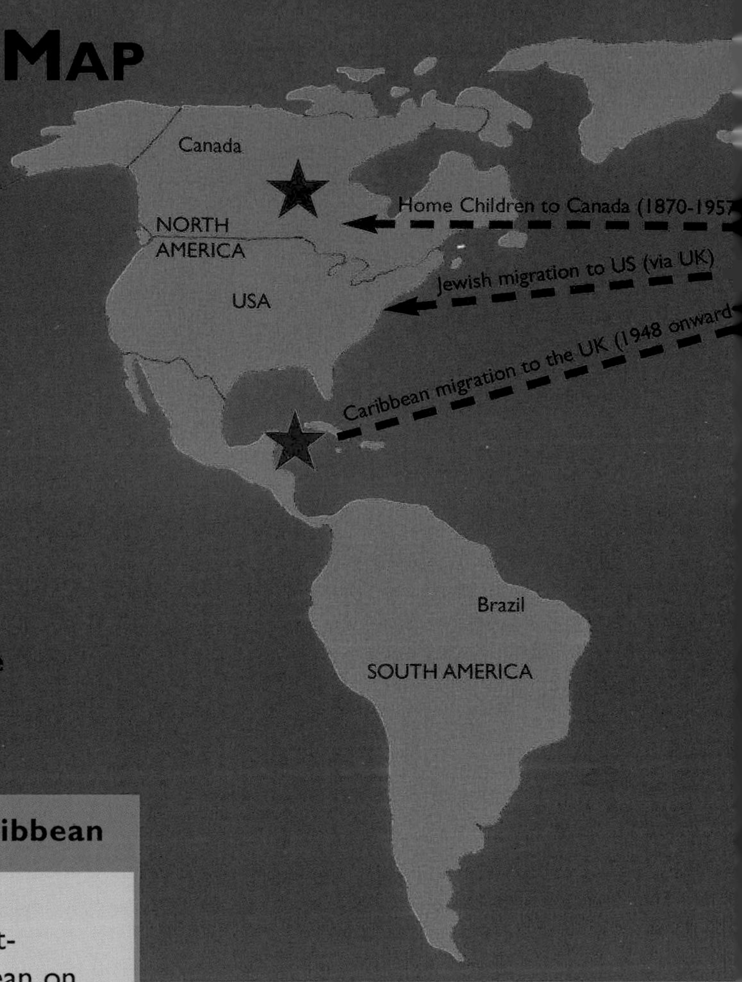

Canada
NORTH AMERICA
USA
Home Children to Canada (1870-1957
Jewish migration to US (via UK)
Caribbean migration to the UK (1948 onward
Brazil
SOUTH AMERICA

Key to Map

★ = case studies

= movement of people

Case Study 2: The Caribbean

Spencer's Visit

Spencer has visited his great-grandparents in the Caribbean on three occasions. He was taken there by his grandmother, who was born and spent her early years in Barbados. Grandma's home was in a rural area with a septic tank and animals roaming free outside.

Grandma told Spencer about the boat she sailed on to England for the first time in the 1960s. The journey took days. He asked her questions about her school friends, and the games she played. He wanted to know about the animals outside her house, and what types of plants grew in her garden. Many things were different from his life in England.

Migration from the Caribbean

From the late sixteenth century many African people were traded as slaves by British, Dutch, French and Brazilian merchants. Many were brought via Britain to its colonies in the Caribbean. The merchants or pirates took slaves by force and sold them for a profit to plantation owners. These owners ran large farms of coffee, bananas, sugar cane, and tobacco which were sent to Britain and sold.

After the Second World War, the British government asked people of the Caribbean if they would come to

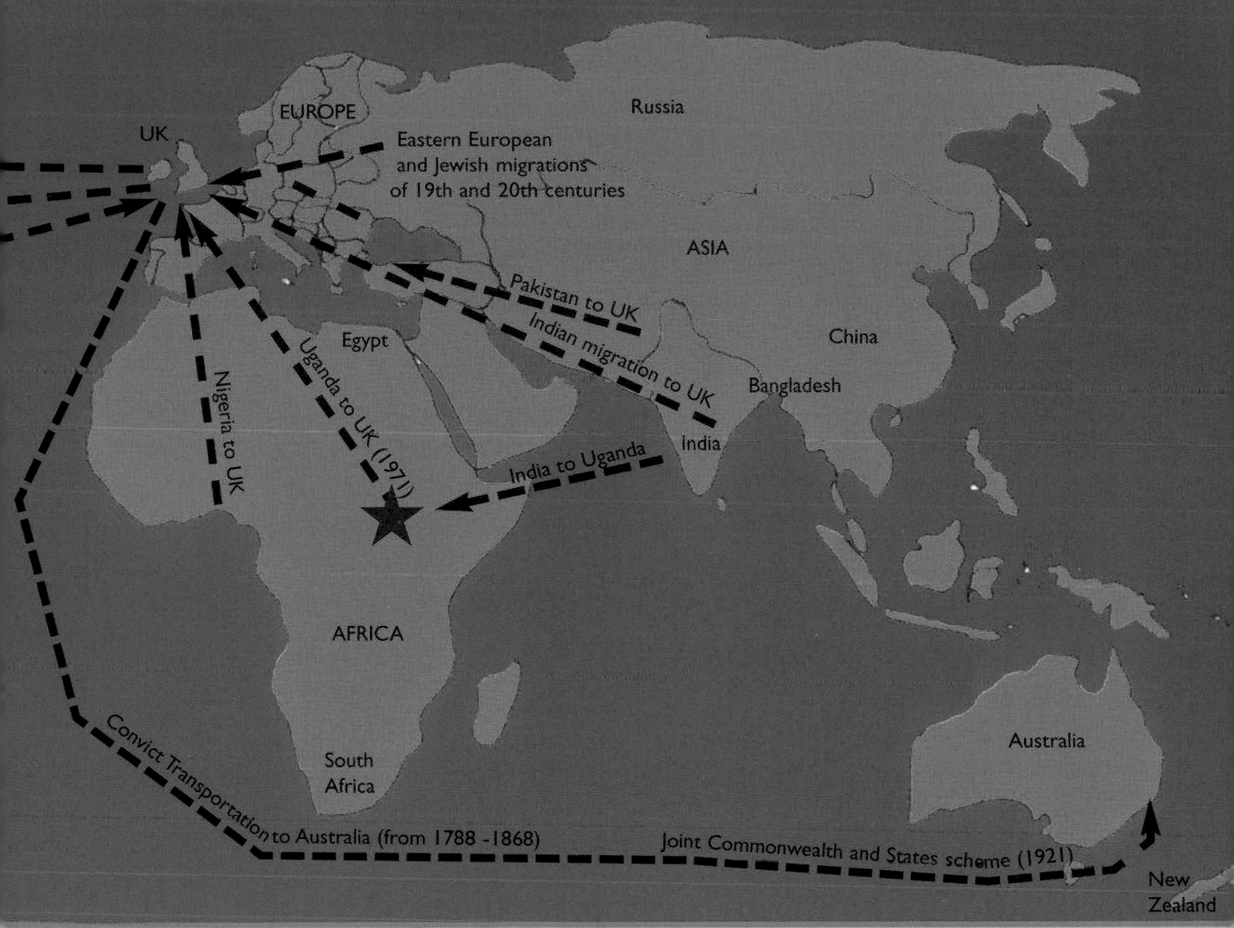

Britain and help reconstruct towns and cities destroyed during the war. Caribbean people served in both World Wars, and some had also stayed on in Britain afterwards.

The first post-war Caribbean immigrants arrived in Britain on the **Empire Windrush** in 1948. Since then, many Caribbean people have settled in Britain.

Read more about...

Migration and Empire.............. see the recommended books list on page 56.

Emigrating to Australia

Although **ABORIGINES** have lived in Australia for centuries, Europeans first visited the country in the seventeenth century and it was 'discovered' by Britain in 1770. A few years later Britain began to worry about its criminals because there was nowhere suitable to keep large numbers of convicts.

Australia was suggested and the **First Fleet** of convicts arrived in 1788 (in a process called **TRANSPORTATION**). They created a camp at Port Jackson (now Sydney). Starvation and disease led

Case Study 3: Canadian Home Child

In the nineteenth century, Britain encouraged poor Britons to settle in Canada. Many Scots and Irish people led the way, encouraged by promises of free land. In 1867, Britain passed the British North America Act, allowing the new federation of Canada to rule itself. However, Canada has always retained close ties with Britain, and many Canadians fought in both World Wars.

George's Story

On 24 March 1904, 12-year-old Londoner, George Stephen Jolly, climbed aboard the steamship *SS Southwark* at Liverpool. George was a **HOME CHILD**: he was being sent to a new home in Canada. Mostly this was due to children being orphans; occasionally their parents were alive, but too poor to look after them.

On 5 April 1904, the ship arrived at Portland. From here, George and others travelled to Toronto.

The distribution home decided where George would be sent. Children were sent to work on isolated farms, as servants, or as apprentices. They were often very frightened, and they had to stay with their employer until the age of 18.

George was one of 100,000 British Home Children who were sent to Canada by over 50 British child care organizations between 1870 and 1957.

to many difficulties, but eventually the colony developed a farm, helped by local Aborigines.

Ex-convicts, and other Britons seeking a new life, settled throughout Australia, building up the country. When gold was found there in the 1850s, there was a rush of people from all over the world.

In the twentieth century, under the 1921 Joint Commonwealth and States Scheme, the British government paid for poorer Britons to travel to Australia to make a new life for themselves and their families.

Jewish Migration

The history of Jewish migration is often linked very closely to periods of persecution.

In the 1860s many Jews fled cholera in Russia and famine in Lithuania. In the 1870s Russia (including Polish Russia) began to move all Jews into **GHETTOES**

Find out more...

For internet links to help trace your ancestors across the world see pages 58-59.

and in 1890 Jewish people were banished from living in Moscow.

As a result of this and other events, 150,000 Jewish immigrants settled in Britain between 1881 and 1914.

Many Jewish people arrived in the port of London, and settled in the East End. Many Jews of this period also travelled through Britain to the USA where they arrived by boat via **ELLIS ISLAND**.

Britain also saw an influx of Jewish people from Germany and Eastern Europe following their persecution in the 1930s and 1940s and the events of the **HOLOCAUST.**

Migration and Britain

Migration has been a fact of life in Britain from its very earliest times and has often contributed to the future of the country. For example, the invasion of the **ANGLO-SAXONS** and **JUTES** in the fifth and sixth centuries AD saw the beginnings of the English language.

Today many people still come to work and live here. In the mid-1990s economic/political issues and wars led many to come from Eastern Europe. Recently, people from new **EU** nations such as Lithuania, Poland, Bulgaria and Romania have sought work in Britain. Their work helps Britain's economy.

Activities: Empire and Migration

- Have any of your living relatives lived or worked abroad? Write down the names of the countries and the jobs they did.

Country	**Job**
....	....
....	....
....	....
....	....

- Do the same for your family's ancestors. Where did they live and what jobs did they do?

Country	**Job**
....	....
....	....
....	....
....	....
....	....

- Put a cross on the map on pages 32-33 to show what you've listed.

- Make a list of all the nationalities in your family tree.

- **British Empire: Two Views**
  Some historians say the British Empire helped many nations and people, that it brought English laws and education, railways and new technologies.

  Other historians say that it was harmful; that it prevented people from earning enough money to live, and that it led to violence.

  Why do you think there are such differing opinions?

My Family in Wartime

Most of us have ancestors who were affected in some way by the First and Second World War. Both changed British life dramatically. Try to find out how your family were affected.

First World War (1914-1918)

There are very few people alive today who remember the First World War. Ask your family about how your ancestors may have been involved.

Opening questions...

- Did anyone in the family fight?
- Was anyone killed? Where are they buried?
- Where did the family live during the war? What jobs did they do?
- What jobs did your female ancestors do for the war effort?

Men were involved in a number of roles during the First World War. They may have been a soldier, a sailor, or part of the **Royal Flying Corps**. Perhaps they served at sea as part of the **Merchant Navy**?

Your female ancestors may have worked as nurses in the many hospitals set up to help the troops. Some women were sent abroad to work as nurses near the battlefields. Many worked in factories making munitions and weapons for the war. This was often very difficult and dangerous work.

If your ancestor was a **Quaker** or a **pacifist**, he may have refused to go to war for ethical reasons. Such people were called **Conscientious objectors** and were often treated badly, imprisoned, humiliated and accused of cowardice.

One of the few ways in which civilians were directly affected by the war was through **zeppelin** air raids. Bombs from the German Zeppelins may have fallen on your ancestors' homes or in their area. These were the first air raids Britain had ever seen.

Did anyone receive a medal?

The Medal Card Index is a very helpful online resource which lists everyone who received a medal during or after the War. It includes nurses officers and ordinary soldiers who served overseas.

- Beware! Many men served in several regiments (some of which may not have been based locally).
- Visit the National Archives website to find the index (**see pages 40-42 and 58-59**).

Gas masks were introduced in the First World War only after many soldiers were killed or made ill by poison gas.

Second World War (1939-1945)

As with the First World War many people served abroad in the Army, Navy and Airforce (RAF). There are many people around today who remember the events of this war. Take care to respect a person's wish not to talk about the war – they may be upset by their memories.

Opening questions...

- Did any of the family fight in the War? If so, where?
- Was anyone taken prisoner?
- Were your family bombed? Was their house destroyed or were family members killed?
- Were any of your ancestors **EVACUATED**?
- Was an ancestor in the Home Guard (see below)?

Home Front

Not all men were able to fight abroad – some were medically unfit, or the wrong age. However, many wanted to do what they could and some of your family may have been members of the **Home Guard**. This was created to protect Britain from any invasion that might occur. Records of the Home Guard are available in local record offices to either those who served or their **NEXT-OF-KIN**.

All 19–40 year old women, without children or husbands at home, were required to register for war work. When the war ended, some women remained in work, often on a part-time basis (see page 27).

Rationing

Food rationing was a part of everyday civilian life during and after the Second World War. This list shows the daily rations per adult:

- twelve ounces of bread,
- six ounces of vegetables,
- a pound of potatoes,
- two ounces of oatmeal,
- an ounce of fat,
- six-tenths of a pint of milk,
- small amounts of cheese, meat, fish, sugar, eggs and dried fruit.
- Eggs were very rare

Read more about food and rationing on page 28.

During the war, everyone (including children) were required to have Identity Cards to help protect national security (see right for a child's card).

Did you know?

- Local newspapers often published detailed obituaries of local soldiers and sailors. Ask at your local library or archive for details (pages 40–42).
- Most service records are still held by the Ministry of Defence. Your relative can write to them and ask for his or her own service record. Or, if they are next-of-kin, ask an adult relative to write for you.

Taking My Research Further

As you have seen, you can find out about your family's history just by asking the right questions and looking at evidence found at home. But what if you want to go a little bit further?

This section provides several practical ways to do in-depth research into your family's history.

You will need an adult's help to accomplish most of the tasks so be prepared to plan ahead carefully and allow plenty of time to achieve your aims.

In this section:

Using the Internet

The internet is a valuable tool in family history research. It gives easy access to much of the information you will need. However there are many things to consider when searching online.

Exploring the internet can be one of the most fun ways to practise family history. Most children find logging on easy. You may even find it easier than some older members of your family!

Adult Supervision

Dangers exist with internet usage, and is it always advisable to explore family history sites with a parent or guardian. Grown-ups are necessary for paying for records, and they can be useful in explaining difficult words or expressions.

Sites and links

Websites vary greatly in the amounts of information they offer you. Some claim to have everything you need but then require details or some form of payment before you can explore further (see **Payments**). These are usually set up by companies for profit.

Other sites can provide you with a list of links which can be a useful gateway to exploring and comparing many different sites.

You will find a list of useful links on pages 58 and 59 of this book. Always ask an adult to help you with your online research.

Is a site useful?
The usefulness of a website depends on what you need to know and how easily you can use the site. It may become obvious very quickly that a site contains little relevant information. For example, its focus may be on family history in another country. Many family history sites are not aimed at children and they can use technical language you are not familiar with.

Other sites may have too many pop-up adverts which can be distracting as well as leading you away from your own research.

In these situations it is always wise to ask an adult and/or find a site that you are more comfortable using.

Chatrooms
Forums and chat-rooms can be useful for beginners to family history, although some can send you in the wrong direction. Arguments have been known to flare up between forum users, and some adults may be impatient with a child asking questions. If you would like to ask questions to other genealogists ask an adult to join the chat forums or mailing-lists on your behalf.

Payments, Details & Downloads
For your own safety never submit any personal details to a site or chatroom. If a site requires you to pay to view information always consider the cost and ask an adult for permission.

Some sites may offer free software to help you in your search. Be very careful when downloading material of any kind and always ask permission from your parent or guardian as downloads could harm your computer.

More information, please!
As you discover your family tree you are likely to think of more and more questions. Your parents and teachers often know the answers to these questions. Even if they are unsure, they will probably know where to look.

Case Study: Safety on the Internet

Spencer and his mother found a variety of ways to stay safe online:

- Check the parental controls on the computer. Security software allows you to set access to different levels of site
- www.thinkuknow.co.uk – the official government site about staying safe online
- They often browse the internet together when looking for information about their family.

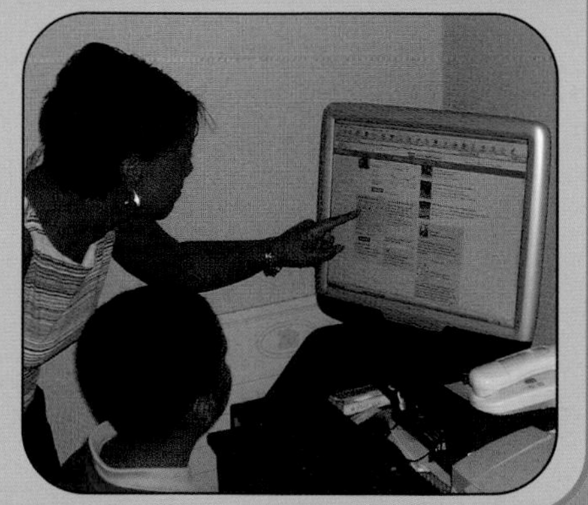

VISITING AN ARCHIVE

Sometimes, the only way of finding out more about your family's past is to visit an archive where large amounts of information about your ancestors may be stored. Ask an adult to help you arrange a visit.

It may be possible to find some records at an **ARCHIVE**, for example at your local record office, museum or library. But some records only exist in larger centres, such as the National Archives. It may also be possible to view the information online. A list of useful archives and their website addresses can be found on page 42.

Do I Need to Visit an Archive?
Ask yourself the following questions before deciding to visit an archive.

- **What am I looking for?**
  Make a list of what information and documents you would like to see when you go. Visit the website of the archive beforehand to find out if they hold the items you need.
- **Do I have to ring or write to arrange a visit?**
  Some archives only open for a few hours each week. It's always best to call and make an appointment.
- **Where is the archive?**
  Is it near, or will you have to travel far? Ask your parent or guardian.
- **Will I need to pay?** Most archives are free, but a few may charge. Always be prepared for costs such as photocopies, lockers, prints from microfilms and photography fees.
- **Do they allow children?**
  Sadly, you will not be able to visit certain archives. Check for age restrictions by calling before you visit. Some places arrange special visits for schools, so ask your teacher if this is possible.

What should I bring?

- A notepad
- Pencil for making notes (pens are not allowed in most archives)
- Money (to pay for photocopies and other materials)

How to Behave
Most archives and libraries have set rules of behaviour:

- Always take care when working with material in the archives. It may be old and fragile.
- Bags: some archives do not allow any kind of bags to be taken into a study area. Lockers will be provided.
- Do not listen to music through headphones or use mobile phones

in archives (turn them off or switch them to silent). Always check if you are allowed to take a photograph on your camera or mobile phone.

- Never use flash photography – flashes can damage some old documents and materials.
- Do not eat snacks or bring drinks into study areas. Food is prohibited from all archives.
- If you find a document difficult to read, ask to have it photocopied. This way you will be able to show it to your parent/guardian or teacher and ask for their help in understanding it.
- Always respect other users' wish for peace and quiet. Thousands of people visit archives every day to work and study family history.

What you could find in your local archives...

There may be several local sources for discovering how your family used to live.

- Ask in your local library for their newspaper holdings – did a member of your family feature in a newspaper report? They may have submitted a marriage entry, or there may be an **OBITUARY**. Perhaps your ancestor raised money for charity, or even committed a crime!

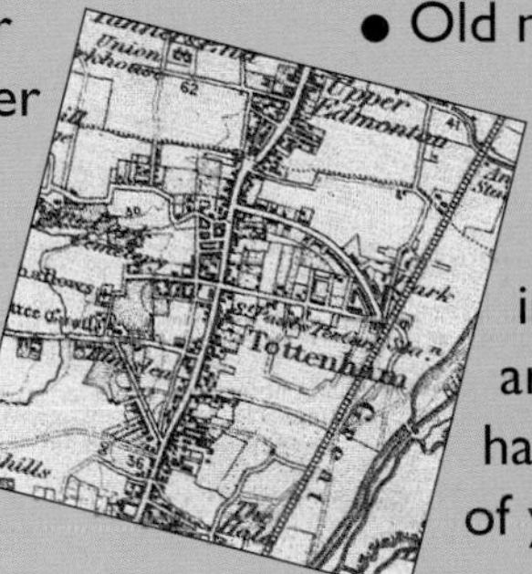

- Old maps can be useful for showing how your home town or village looked in past times. The archive may also have photographs of your house, street or neighbourhood.

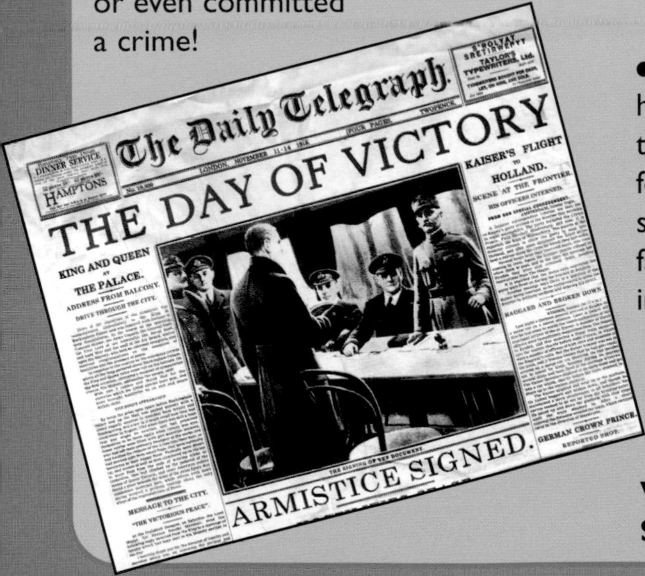
The Daily Telegraph
THE DAY OF VICTORY
KAISER'S FLIGHT TO HOLLAND.
KING AND QUEEN AT THE PALACE.
ARMISTICE SIGNED.
GERMAN CROWN PRINCE REPORTED SHOT.

- Sometimes archives have collections of the types of paper records found at home – school certificates, family Bibles or inscribed hymn books.

- Check to see if your local studies library has put their collections online.

Where's my nearest archive? See page 42.

How to find your nearest local studies centre.

- Contact your Council and ask about study centres/archives in the area.
- Look on your council website www.[name of council].gov.uk
- Ask at your local library.
- Ask at local history library.
- Ask a parent, grandparent, or school teacher for help.
- Check www.familia.org.uk (a web-based directory of family history resources).

UK and Ireland Archives of Interest

You may not be able to visit all of the archives listed. If you need information from an archive, but cannot visit, ask a member of your family to go on your behalf. You can check the online catalogues and help plan the visit.

- **The National Archives**
Kew, Richmond, Surrey, TW9 4DU
Tel: 020 8876 3444 **Web:** www.nationalarchives.gov.uk
Good for: military records, free access to The Times and CENSUSES online, pre-1858 PCC wills

- **The National Library of Wales**
Aberystwyth, Ceredigion, Wales SY23 3BU
Tel: 01970 632 800 **Web:** www.llgc.org.uk
Good for: information on Welsh ancestors

- **London Probate Department**
PRFD, First Avenue House, 42-49 High Holborn Ground Floor, Holborn, London WC1V 6NP
Tel: 020 7947 6983 **Web:** www.hmcourts-service.gov.uk
Good for: finding and ordering wills from all over England and Wales from 1858 to the present

- **Scotland's People Centre**
General Register Office for Scotland, New Register House, 3 West Register Street, Edinburgh EH1 3YT
Web: www.scotlandspeoplehub.gov.uk/
Good for: tracing Scottish ancestors

- **Public Record Office of Northern Ireland (PRONI)** 66 Balmoral Avenue, Belfast BT9 6NY
Tel: 0289 0255 905 **Web:** www.proni.gov.uk
Good for: tracing Northern Irish ancestors

- **National Archives of Ireland, The National Archives** Bishop Street, Dublin 8, Ireland
Tel: 353 (0)1 407 2300 **Web:** www.nationalarchives.ie
Good for: Irish censuses, Irish property records, and Irish birth, marriage and death (**BMD**) records

- **LDS (Church of the Latter Day Saints) Family History Centres**
100 in the UK – there is probably one near you.
Web: www.familysearch.org
Good for: church records, Irish records in the UK, and Caribbean records in the UK

- **Local or County Record Offices**
(LRO or CROs) Ask your parent or teacher to help you find your nearest record office.
Good for: trade directories, local newspapers, ratebooks, land and property records

- **Society of Genealogists**
14 Charterhouse Buildings, Goswell Road, London EC1M 7BA
Tel: 020 7251 8799 **Web:** www.sog.org.uk
Good for: school and university records; occupational records, non-conformist records

- **Local Library**
Ask your parent or teacher about your local library
Good for: local directories, telephone books, free online access, local newspapers

- **Guildhall Library** Aldermanbury, City of London EC2P 7HH **Tel:** 020 7332 1862 or 1863
www.cityoflondon.gov.uk – good for apprenticeship records and City of London ancestors

- **British Library**, London
Tel: 0870 444 1500 **Web:** http://indiafamily.bl.uk/UI
Good for: Finding out about British and Indian ancestors in India; see www.indiafamily.bl.uk

PROJECT SHEETS

On these pages, you will find several suggested project sheets linked to the family history themes in this book. If necessary, ask an adult to help you.

For some of the activities you will need to fill in the boxes on the page. If you want your family or friends to fill in the sheets too you can copy the individual project pages.

You may need to go out or visit places for some projects. Ask your parents if they will take you. Perhaps you could ask your teacher to arrange a visit as part of a school trip?

If you can't visit the places suggested, try writing to the museums or other addresses and asking them to send details to you. Use the information you receive to fill in the boxes on the project pages.

All the projects are linked to themes already covered in the book. This link is shown by the Project Sheet (PS) symbol (see right). Look out for it when reading the pages. When you have finished a project, look back to the linked page and check what you have learned.

PROJECT 1

Creating a Surname Map

(see also pages 8 and 9)

Create a Surname Map for your surname. Put all the locations where your surname can be found on a map. This will show the distribution of your name across the country. Draw the map yourself or print it off from a computer.

What you'll need

- Surname maps can be found on the internet at:
  www.spatial-literacy.org/
  www.rootsmap.com/
  (this is a paying site)
- An atlas
- Pencil or pen

Useful Sources

- Telephone books
- Census records – for example, try the 1881 census at: www.familysearch.org

PROJECT 2

Searching for Ancestors (see also pages 16 and 17)

Try searching an online census.

- How many people can you find with exactly the same name as you?
- How old were they, and what did they do? Write their details below.
- Do you know if you are related to any of them?

If you can't find anyone with your name, try the name of a friend or someone in your family. Try a slightly different spelling of your name.

AGE	JOB
....	....
....	....
....	....
....	....
....	....
....	....

Emma's Example

I searched for 'Emma Jolly' and found 75. However, some of these were spelt 'JOLLEY'. The site also included people called AMY instead of EMMA.

The records that gave an occupation included a Cotton **CARDER**, Cotton **WEAVER**, Frame Tenter (Cotton), Harp Teacher, Brushmaker, Thatcher's Wife, Dairy Woman, Farmer's Girl, Domestic Servant, Dressmaker, Marine Store Dealer, Cook, Licensed Victualler's Wife, and a Packer of Preserved Meats.

- Imagine what it would be like to work in the jobs of your namesakes.

PROJECT 3

Jobs in the Family (see also pages 20-23)

Make a list of all the jobs people in your family do now – e.g. your parents, aunts, uncles, cousins, grandparents etc. Include part-time jobs and jobs done for pocket money.

RELATIVE	CURRENT JOB
....	....
....	....
....	....
....	....
....	....
....	....
....	....
....	....
....	....

Have these jobs always existed? Some jobs may be different due to changes in technology (the use of computers) or new ways of doing the same thing. Try to find how the work in these jobs has changed over the years.

Make a poster
Draw a picture of one of your relatives doing his or her job.

Would you have liked to do this job?

PROJECT 4 PS4

Food from the Past (see also pages 28 and 29)

Where did your ancestors live in the nineteenth century? Were they in the countryside or in the town? What kind of food do you think they had access to? How could you find out? Write the types of food below.

TOWN	COUNTRY
....	....
....	....
....	....
....	....

HINTS

- Old maps and directories might show the locations of shops.
- Looks for information about the kinds of crops grown in the countryside near where they lived.

Using your local library or school internet find and make some recipes from different times and cultures. You could also check old local newspapers in an archive for recipes and ideas.

Rationing (see also pages 28 and 37)

- Consider the rations listed on page 37. What kind of meals could you make? How could you make the food go further?

Did You Know?
Bacon, butter and sugar were the first items to be rationed in 1940. Rationing did not officially end in Britain until 1954.

PROJECT 5 PS5

Wartime Ancestors (see also pages 36 and 37)

How many of your ancestors were soldiers, sailors or airmen?

(i) What were their names?

(ii) When were they born?

(iii) When did they die?

NAME	BIRTH	DEATH	SERVED IN (e.g. Army)
....	....	....	....
....	....	....	....
....	....	....	....
....	....	....	....

(iv) Can you think of ways to discover more about them?

HINTS

- Ask living relatives.
- Try to find out if they won any medals (see below).
- Look at old copies of local newspapers in your library.
- Are there any photos of soldiers or sailors in the family album? What can the photo tell you? (See pages 12 and 13 for more hints on how to look for useful details in a photograph.)

Did you know?

On www.nationalarchives.gov.uk you can search documents online for your ancestor's First World War medal card. Simply put his surname and first initial into the boxes and click search. If you already know his regiment, put that in too. The results also include officers.

Caution!

It is possible that your ancestor served in several regiments. Also, the regiment he served in might not have been based locally.

PROJECT 6 PS6

Historical Re-enactments (see also pages 20-23 and 60)

Find out where a historical re-enactment, special museum event, battlefield walk, or past times fair is happening near you. Look in local newspapers, event listing magazines or on the internet.

Try:
www.countyfetes.co.uk
www.battlefieldstrust.com
www.ncm.org.uk
www.nrm.org.uk
www.electricscotland.com/kids/
www.themcs.org

- Take photos and make notes on what you see at a re-enactment.
- How historically accurate are the costumes and the activities? Using your school history text books, list reasons why they are or are not accurate.

ACCURATE	NOT ACCURATE
....	....
....	....
....	....

- Do you think that any of your ancestor wore clothes like these? (Your ability to answer this will rely on how far you have been able to trace your family back and the type of re-enactment/museum you have visited.)
- Make a poster of the photos you have taken.

PROJECT 7 PS7

Records for the Future: Your Place in History

History is being created right now. You need to note down what is happening so that it is recorded for the future. Try these three projects:

1) Make a scrapbook of your life.
This will help your descendants to find out about you. Think about how you might organise it: you could make a dfferent book for each year or split it into themes. Ask your brothers and sisters to make one too.

Put in photographs of you, your friends and your family.

Include facts about you and your life.

Stick in artwork that you have made and documents that mean something to you. Don't forget that you can include copies. If a document is very delicate or precious, it is better to ask an adult to photocopy it for you.

2) Make a box documents all about your life

- Tickets to plays or concerts you have attended
- Magazine images of your favourite bands or pop stars
- Flyers for events
- Copies of your school report
- Invitations to parties
- Sports badges or certificates
- Music certificates
- Maps of your town or village

3) Write a questionnaire about yourself

Potential questions could be:
- What is your full name?
- When were you born?
- Where do you live?
- Who is your best friend?
- What do you like to eat?
- Where do you go to school?
- What hobbies do you have?
- Where are going on holiday this year?

Did You Know?
When you are older, you can pull out the scrapbook and remember how you used to be.

Glossary of Terms

This section further explains terms from earlier in the book. It also covers words you may find during your family history research.

Act of Union - (1707) Parliamentary Act that united England and Scotland as Great Britain.

Adoption - placing a child with a guardian other than the birth mother or father. Before 1927, there was no official adoption service and no formal records. and so the Adopted Children's Register was created. An adopted child can access it when he or she becomes 18 (16 in Scotland).

Aborigines - the first inhabitants of Australia.

Agricultural Revolution - period of farming development in Britain that led to massive increases in productivity.

American War of Independence (1775-1883) - war between Britain and thirteen colonies of the North American continent, resulting in the declaration of the United States of America (USA) in 1776.

Anglo-Saxons - term used to describe people of South and East Britain in the 5th century who were descended from the Angle and Saxon Germanic tribes.

Apprentice - a trainee craftsperson.

Archive - a place where public records are stored e.g. library.

Asylum (page 26) - a hospital specialising in the care of people with mental illnesses.

Asylum (page 31) - a process by which a person, persecuted for their beliefs or opinions in his/her country, can claim protection in another country.

Bachelor - an unmarried man.

'Base' child or **'base born'** (see **illegitimacy**).

Biographical Dictionary - a book containing information about notable people in society.

Birth Certificate - paper record of a birth registered with the **GRO**.

BMD - (Birth, Marriage and **Death)** Certificates for BMDs were first introduced in 1837.

British Colonial Office - a government department, created in 1854, to run the British colonies.

Carder - someone who combs wool to align the fibres (see also **spinning**).

Census - the collection of information and statistics about every household in the country that takes place every ten years. The census as we know it today started in 1801. The most useful censuses for family historians in England and Wales are those for 1841, 1851, 1861, 1871, 1881, 1891 and 1901. Scotland has separate censuses for the same years. Many of Ireland's census records were destroyed but some do survive. The 1901 and 1911 censuses for Ireland are probably the most useful. The 1841 census for England and Wales was the first to record the names of everyone in each household.

Cereals - a type of grain used for food, such as wheat, maize or barley.

Chapman County Codes - 3 letter abbreviations for counties that existed until 1974 (e.g. NFK for Norfolk).

CHURCH OF ENGLAND - the official Church of England since the 16th Century when it broke away from Roman Catholicism during the Reformation.

CIVILIAN - a non-military person.

CIVIL REGISTRATION - a legal system of recording all births, marriages, and deaths. The Registration Act and Marriage Act were passed in 1836. From 1837, all births, marriages and deaths should have been registered and certificates issued. However, some still went unregistered. From 1875, non-registration was illegal, and punishable by fines.

CLASS MOBILITY - the ease with which people can move between classes.

COLD WAR - period of tension and competition (1945-1990s) between the United States and the Soviet Union without any direct military action between the two sides.

COMMONWEALTH OF NATIONS - a group of countries, formerly members of the the British Empire.

CONSCIENTIOUS OBJECTOR - a person who, due to their beliefs, will not serve in a time of war.

CONVICT - a convicted criminal.

CRO - County Record Office.

DEATH CERTIFICATES give the name, age and occupation of the deceased, the date and place of death, the cause of death, and the name, occupation and residence of the informant. These help with a medical family history, and give you further information on people in your **FAMILY TREE**.

DEPRESSION - (the Great Depression - 1930s) an economic slump with many people unemployed.

DIASPORA - the spread of a people or country's population across the world.

DIG FOR VICTORY - a campaign during the **SECOND WORLD WAR** which encouraged citizens to grow their own fruit and vegetables. This helped combat the food shortage of the time.

DIOCESE - a region of churches overseen by a Bishop.

DISCRIMINATION - making a (usually unfair) choice based on a difference between people (e.g. race, disability or sex).

DIVORCE - the legal end of a marriage; when a married couple separate legally.

DRIPPING - animal fat collected into a jar from the meat cooked at home.

'DROPT' CHILD - See **FOUNDLING** or **ILLEGITIMATCY**.

EAST INDIA COMPANY - an English Company which traded in Indian goods. The Company became the main administrative rulers of India, until 1858, when control moved to the British government.

EEC - European Economic Community. Formed in 1957, it was renamed European Union (**EU**) in 1992.

ELLIS ISLAND - main entry point for immigrants to the USA between 1892 and 1954.

EMIGRATION - moving away from your country of origin to live elsewhere.

EMPIRE WINDRUSH - a ship that arrived in Britain in June 1949 carrying 492 Jamaican people - the first large group of West Indian immigrants since the end of the war.

Enumerators - people who collect information for the **census**.

Evacuee/Evacuation - Wartime process (especially in Second World War) of sending children to live in safer areas of the country.

EU - European Union.

Expatriates - former members of one country living in another country.

Family History - the practise of studying and discovering a family's past (see also **Genealogy**).

Family Tree - a chart showing members of a family and how they are related.

Famine - Lack of food leading to starvation (and often death) of people.

First Fleet - the first 11 ships that sailed to New South Wales, Australia from Britain in 1787. This marked the start of **transportation**.

First World War - The Great War of 1914-1918; also known as 'the war to end all wars'.

Foundling - a baby abandoned by its parent(s), often as a result of poverty or other difficulties. There are few records of the parents of foundlings, but there are some records from institutions (such as Thomas Coram's Foundling Hospital in London). Since 1977, foundlings have been recorded in the Register of Abandoned Children.

Game - the meat of wild birds, animals or fish that have been hunted for food or sport (e.g. boar, pheasant, venison).

Genealogy - the study of ancestry; the **pedigree** produced by such study.

Generation - people who are born and live around the same period in history; those produced by the same parents (in a **pedigree** chart/**family tree**).

Ghetto - an area populated by a minority group, usually a segregated area (e.g. the Jewish Ghettoes in Nazi Europe).

Gregorian Calendar - the current system for organising days of the year.

GRO - General Register Office.

Harvest time - the season when ripe grain and other edible produce are collected (there may be several harvests a year, depending on what is grown).

Heir - the person who receives the property or title of the previous owner (e.g. Heir to the Crown).

Heraldry - the study of coats of arms and their uses in **genealogy**.

Holocaust - the mass murder of six million Jewish people in the late 1930s and during the **Second World War**.

Home Child - term describing orphaned and unwanted British children sent to Canada between 1850 and 1957.

Home Guard - a volunteer group of men, otherwise ineligible for military service, who defended Britain between 1940 and 1944.

House of Lords - the upper house of the UK Parliament.

Hops - fruit of the hop-plant; used in the production of beer and malt liquors.

Illegitimacy - an old-fashioned and slightly offensive term, meaning that a child was born without his/her parents being married.

Immigration - the process of entering

a country and (usually) becoming a permanent resident.

INDEPENDENCE - process (for a country) of breaking free from the control of another country.

INDUSTRIAL REVOLUTION - a period of economic, social and technological change (especially in industry) in Britain from 1780 to the 1840s.

INDUSTRIALISTS - manufacturers, or those who manage or own an industry.

INNS OF COURT - the professsional association to which every barrister must belong. The fours Inns are based in London. The **INNS OF CHANCERY** were the buildings of these associations until the nineteenth century.

INSTITUTION - many ancestors can be shown on censuses as living in institutions. This could be a school, hospital, army barracks, prison, or workhouse.

JUTE - a fibre used to make ropes, canvas, sacking etc.; a product taken from the jute plants of West Bengal in India and modern Bangladesh.

KIPPER - typically, a preserved herring or salmon was known as a kipper.

LANDED GENTRY - a member of the wealthier classes who owned land; usually lower in social class than Peers or others with titles (e.g. Duke).

LATIN - an ancient language, used by the Romans and in some legal documents in England (up to 1732).

LAW LIST - the directory of lawyers, law firms and related legal services.

LICENCE (also **lic**. Or **ML**) - most ancestors married by Banns. Sometimes people married by Licence.

LRO - Local Record Office

MAIDEN NAME - the surname of a woman before she is married.

MARRIAGE CERTIFICATES are also helpful. They give the full names of the bride and groom, their ages, their addresses, their occupations, the names of the witnesses, and the names and occupations of their fathers. These documents provide a very useful way of confirming the names of the parents of a married couple.

MASTER - the teacher of an apprentice; the most experienced at his craft.

MERCHANT NAVY/SEAMEN - men who served on commercial or trading ships.

MIDDLE AGES - the period in history between the Ancient Times (of the Greeks etc.) and the Modern Period (beginning in 15th/16th centuries).

MIGRATION (see **IMMIGRATION** and **EMIGRATION**) - movement of peoples between lands and nations.

MILLING - working in a Mill (often cotton and wool mills).

MONUMENTAL INSCRIPTION (MI) - the inscription on a grave or tombstone.

MUNITIONS - weapons.

MUTTON - meat from an older sheep.

NATURAL CHILD - see **ILLEGITIMACY.**

NAZI - a member of the National Socialist German Worker's Party (1933-1945), led by Adolph Hitler.

NONCONFORMIST - a person who did not conform to the established religion. In the 19th and 20th centuries the established religion of England and Wales was the **CHURCH OF ENGLAND**

(or Anglican Church). Roman Catholics, Jews, Quakers, Unitarians, Methodists, Baptists and members of other faiths were described as 'Nonconformist'.

Oatmeal - a product made from ground oats; used to make biscuits, porridge and oatcakes.

Obituary - a record of a death (usually in a newspaper), often including a short biography of the life of the deceased.

Old French - language spoken in northern half of modern France between 1000 and 1300 AD.

Pacifist - a person completely opposed to war or violence.

Parish - a small section of a county.

Parish registers - a record of baptisms, marriages and burials for a specific parish; some registers include birth and death dates; usually the registers are kept at the local record office, but some are retained by the church.

Patronymic - a surname based on the name of a person's father.

Partition of Ireland - the separation of Northern Ireland from the state of Ireland.

Pedigrees - family trees (sometimes with further description of ancestry); some are published. You must be very careful when looking at research someone else has done. Ask yourself what sources were used, and how? Where is the proof? Many people accept prepared family trees without question. Be careful! Many are wrong.

Poaching (see also **Game**) - taking game or fish illegally (usually by trespassing on the land of others).

Pogrom - a form of riot (often violent) directed against a particular group.

Probate - the proving of a will (when the contents of the will can be distributed by the executors).

Protectorate - an area that agrees, by treaty, to be controlled by another, usually more powerful, country.

Pulses - legumes (e.g. peas, lentils, beans).

Quakers - a religious group founded in the seventeenth century.

RAF - Royal Air Force.

Rationing - (in **Second World War**) a process where each person had a set allowance (or ration) of food, clothes, and fuel.

Registrar - an official (usually from the local council) who keeps records, especially of Births, Marriages and Deaths (see **BMD**).

Registration District - an area used by administrators of Civil Registration and the Census to divide England, Wales

Relations

First Cousin - the son or daughter of your uncle or aunt (the **sibling** of your parent).

First Cousin Once Removed - the son or daughter of your first cousin OR the son or daughter of your great uncle or aunt.

Great Uncle or Aunt - the brother or sister of your grandparent.

Second Cousin - the son or daughter of your first cousin once removed.

and Scotland. These were divided into subdistricts. It is important to note which registration district your ancestor lived in so that you know where to search in indexes.

ROYAL FLYING CORPS - the airforce of the British military during the First World War. It became the **RAF** in 1918.

SCAPEGOAT - a person or group who is blamed falsely for a problem or mistake.

SECOND WORLD WAR - a global conflict that began in Europe in 1939 and which ended in Europe in May 1945 and in Asia in August 1945 (with the use of the first atomic bombs).

SIBLING - a brother or sister.

SLAVERY - a system under which people (known as slaves) are deprived of freedom, traded as good and made to perform work for no payment.

SPINNING - a process of drawing out thread from wool and so on to prepare it for use in making clothes.

SPINSTER - an unmarried woman.

STRAW PLAITING - an old rural craft where straw was plaited and sold for decoration or use in products, like hats.

SUFFRAGE - the right to vote in political elections.

SUFFRAGETTE - name given to the women who campaigned and protested for women's suffrage in the early twentieth century.

TNA - The National Archives

TRANSPORTATION - the process of sending convicts to a penal colony (e.g. Britain to Australia in the 18th and 19th centuries).

TRIPE - the stomach of a cow; or the intestines of a pig or fish eaten as food.

U-BOATS - (*Unterseeboot* or Under sea boat); German and Austrian submarines used to target Allied shipping (especially merchant ships) during both world wars.

UNION - several parishes formed into a Union to administer the poor laws.

UNPASTEURISED MILK - milk that has not been pasteurised (or heat treated) to kill bacteria.

URBAN - relating to a town or city.

WALL STREET CRASH (1929) - the largest fall in the value of the US stock market in history often regarded as the start of the **DEPRESSION**.

WEAVER - a person who makes cloth.

WIDOW - a woman whose husband has died.

WIDOWER - a man whose wife has died.

WILL - a legal document describing how a person wishes to dispose of his or her property after his or her death.

WORKHOUSE - an institution providing indoor and outdoor relief for the poor of the parish or **UNION**.

ZEPPELIN - a type of airship used to bomb British towns and cities during the **FIRST WORLD WAR**.

Recommended Reading

The following books will help expand your knowledge of the themes in this book.

Younger Readers

Jobs

The Worst Children's Jobs in History by Tony Robinson

The Little Princess by Frances Hodgson Burnett

Class

Remember the Lusitania! by Diana Preston

Victorian Workhouse (My Story) by Pamela Oldfield

Women

Jane Eyre by Charlotte Brontë

The Railway Children by Edith Nesbit

War

Terry Deary's Terribly True War Stories

The Silver Sword by Ian Seraillier

Goodnight Mister Tom by Michelle Magorian

Migration

Out of the Hitler Time by Judith Kerr

Empire

The Secret Garden by Frances Hodgson Burnett

Walkabout by James Vance Marshall

Research

Britannia: 100 Great Stories from British History by Geraldine McCaughrean

Our Island Story by H.E. Marshall

Older Readers

Jobs

The Midwife's Apprentice by Karen Cushman

A Christmas Carol by Charles Dickens

Class

Coram Boy by Jamila Gavin

Flambards by K M Peyton

Women

Pride and Prejudice by Jane Austen

A Question of Courage by Marjorie Darke

War

The Diary of a Young Girl by Anne Frank

The Guns of Easter by Gerard Whelan

The Machine Gunners by Robert Westall

Migration and Empire

The Growth of the British Empire by M B Synge

Under the Hawthorn Tree: Children of the Famine by Marita Conlon-McKenna

Research

Re-discovering the Making of the UK: Britain, 1500-1750 (Rediscovering the Past) by Colin Shepherd

The Story of London by Richard Brassey

Films to Watch

Emma, 1996 (Regency era)

Great Expectations, 1948 (Victorian era)

The Railway Children, 1970 (Edwardian era)

The Kidnappers, 1953 (Edwardian era in Canada)

Lawrence of Arabia, 1962 (First World War)

All Quiet on the Western Front, 1930

Chariots of Fire, 1981 (1920s)

Empire of the Sun, 1987 (World War II)

Hope and Glory, 1987 (World War II)

Carrie's War, 1974 (World War II)

Gandhi, 1982 (Indian independence)

Recommended Museums

Visit websites of these museums to get contact details and find out what they hold.

Bethnal Green Museum of Childhood History of childhood and children's artefacts: www.museumofchildhood.org.uk

Black Country Living Museum Everyday life in the industrial West Midlands: www.bclm.co.uk

Blists Hill and Ironbridge (Shropshire) An open-air museum about the beginnings of the Industrial Revolution: www.ironbridge.org.uk

British Empire & Commonwealth Museum (Bristol) A family-friendly museum looking at all aspects of Empire and Commonwealth history – the good and the bad: www.empiremuseum.co.uk

Castle Museum (York) One of the best UK museums of everyday life in the past: www.yorkcastlemuseum.org.uk

Cobh Heritage Centre, (Co Cork, Ireland) Records of both internal and international Irish migration: www.cobhheritage.com

Dicken's World (Kent) Museum based on Dicken's life, it recreates the sights, sounds and smells of Victorian England: www.dickensworld.co.uk

Geffrye Museum (London) Reconstructions of period homes from the 16th century: www.geffrye-museum.org.uk

Imperial War Museum (London) Wars of the British Empire, especially good on the Second World War: www.iwm.org.uk

Imperial War Museum North (Manchester): www.iwm.org.uk

International Slavery Museum (Liverpool) Includes many untold stories of slaves throughout history: www.liverpoolmuseums.org.uk/ism/

Museum of London The history of London: www.museumoflondon.org.uk

National Army Museum (London) All aspects of British Army history: www.national-army-museum.ac.uk/

National Coal Museum (Cardiff) Useful for finding out about the lives of mining ancestors: www.museumwales.ac.uk/en/bigpit/

National Trust Back-To-Back Houses, (Birmingham) Restored 19th century working-class homes in one of Britain's most important industrial cities. Follow links at: www.nationaltrust.org.uk

People's History Museum (Manchester) National museum for the history of working people in Britain: www.phm.org.uk/

RAF Museum (Hendon, London and Cosford, Shropshire) Explore the aircraft used by RAF & RFC ancestors: www.rafmuseum.org.uk/

Regimental Museums To find the specific regiment you need go to: www.regiments.org

The Royal Navy Museum (Portsmouth Dockyard) The history of Britain's Naval exploits: www.royalnavalmuseum.org

Scotland Street School Museum (Glasgow) Scotland's educational history in a classroom experience. Follow links at: www.glasgowmuseums.com

Ulster Folk and Transport Museum (County Down, N Ireland) Traditional life in Northern Ireland's past: www.uftm.org.uk

The Way We Were (Lancashire) Life inside a Victorian classroom. Follow links at: www.wlct.org/Tourism/Wiganpier/wiganpier.htm

Internet Sources

Some of the following sites may require payment. They may be free to access in full at some libraries and record offices (e.g. www.ancestry.co.uk).

General Family History

www.familysearch.org
www.familyrecords.gov.uk
www.freebmd.org.uk
www.genuki.org.uk
www.freecen.org.uk
www.freereg.org.uk
www.cyndislist.com
www.rootsweb.com
www.bbc.co.uk/history/forkids

Surnames

www.genuki.org.uk/indexes/SurnamesLists.html

Looking at Documents

www.nationalarchives.gov.uk/documentsonline
www.censusfinder.com/
www.familysearch.org
www.ancestry.co.uk
www.thegenealogist.co.uk
www.findmypast.com
www.1901censusonline.com
www.gazettes-online.co.uk

Family Tree

www.bbc.co.uk/history/familyhistory/ (includes tips on how to draw your tree)

Timeline

www.british-history.ac.uk
www.visionofbritain.org.uk
www.historicaldirectories.org
http://freepages.genealogy.rootsweb.com/~genmaps

Jobs

http://homepage.ntlworld.com/hitch/gendocs/trades.html
www.hevanet.com/gladhaus/tradeslist.html (list of old jobs found in British censuses and parish records)

Class

www.booth.lse.ac.uk (London Poverty Maps)
www.workhouses.org.uk (learn about workhouse conditions)
www.collectbritain.co.uk (British Library sound archive: listen to the different accents of the past)

Ancestors Across the World

www.movinghere.org (good for Afro-Caribbean, Asian and Jewish family history sources)
www.ellisisland.org/ (for US immigrants)
www.learningcurve.gov.uk/empire (children's learning site)
www.worldgenweb.org
www.jewishgen.org
www.jgsgb.org.uk (Jewish Genealogical Society of Great Britain: restricted access information on Jewish immigrants)
www.imagesofempire.com
www.ancestorsonboard.com (passenger lists (paying site)
www.understandingslavery.com

Military & War

www.regiments.org (details on all British and overseas troop regiments)

www.nationalarchives.gov.uk (Research Guides on all military service records)
www.iwm.org.uk (Imperial War Museum)
www.national-army-museum.ac.uk (The National Army Museum)
www.royalnavalmuseum.org (The Royal Navy Museum)
www.rafmuseum.org.uk (The Royal Air Force Museum)

First World War

www.learningcurve.gov.uk/greatwar (children's learning site)
www.roll-of-honour.com/Databases/
www.cwgc.org (names of those who died in the First World War)
www.channel4.com/history/microsites/L/lostgeneration/
www.1914-1918.net (detailed information on where regiments were serving)

Second World War

www.learningcurve.gov.uk/homefront/ (resources on the home front, specifically for children)
www.mansell.com/pow-index.html (POWs in Japanese Camps)
www.nationalarchives.gov.uk (Second World War internees' files & indexes)
www.holocausteducationaltrustireland.org (Holocaust information for children)

Archives

www.archivesmadeeasy.org
www.gro.gov.uk (the official site of the General Register Office)
www.nationalarchives.gov.uk (links to a2a and Archon (lists of records and respositories throughout the country)
www.groireland.ie and www.groni.gov.uk (General Register Offices in Dublin and Belfast)
www.proni.gov.uk (Public Record Office of Northern Ireland)
www.irishorigins.com
www.familysearch.org (the Latter Day Saints have collections of Irish records at their family history centres across Britain and the world)

Scottish Genealogy

www.scotlandspeople.gov.uk/ (paying site with a very good range of online records, including censuses, Old Parochial Registers, Birth, Marriage and Death certificates and Wills)
www.nas.gov.uk/ (National Archives of Scotland)
www.scotsgenealogy.com (Scottish Genealogical Society)
www.ancestry.co.uk (indexes only to Scottish censuses)

Welsh Genealogy

www.llgc.org.uk (National Library of Wales)
www.genuki.org.uk (good information on Welsh parishes and spelling differences)

Irish Genealogy

www.irishancestry.com (free to search)
www.ireland.com/ancestor

Educational Links and Resources

www.nationalarchives.gov.uk/teachers/kids.htm (features games and activities for children)
www.learningcurve.gov.uk (site for children studying history at school)

LINKS TO SCHOOL WORK

Many of the topics covered in this book are relevant to the National History Curriculum for Key Stages 2 (7-11 year olds) and 3 (11-14 year olds). Look out for these symbols: 2 3

The table below shows which sections of the book will help to raise awareness of different periods and aspects of history covered in school lessons.

Family History Topics

Page	Area	Relates to:
8-9	My Family Surname	**KEY STAGE 2:** Local History
10-11	Interviewing My Family	**KEY STAGE 2:** Britain since 1930; local history
12-15	Looking at My Photos and Documents	**KEY STAGE 3:** analysing historical data
16-17	My Family Tree	**KEY STAGE 2:** Dates
18-19	Timeline	**KEY STAGE 2 & 3:** Kings and Queens; Dates
20-23	Jobs	**KEY STAGE 2:** Victorian Britain - Children's jobs in Victorian Britain (e,g. straw plaiter, cotton factories **KEY STAGE 3:** Agricultural Revolution; Industrial Revolution
24-25	Class	**KEY STAGE 2:** Looking at different political and social viewpoints
26-27	Women	**KEY STAGE 2:** understanding political & social differences
28-29	Food	**KEY STAGE 3:** Rationing for your ancestors
32-33	Migration Map	**KEY STAGE 2:** understanding and locating different societies **KEY STAGE 3:** British Empire & Exploration
32-34	Ancestors Around the World	**KEY STAGE 2:** Looking at different political, religious and social viewpoints
36	First World War	**KEY STAGE 3:** First World War
37	Second World War	**KEY STAGE 3:** Second World War; Evacuee ancestors

INDEX

For specific terms see the glossary on pages 50-56.

About the Author

Emma Jolly trained as an historian at the University of Sussex. She holds the IHGS Higher Certificate in Genealogy, and now works as a researcher for her own genealogy company (Genealogic). Her writing has featured in a number of family history journals. Emma lives in London with her husband and two small children.

Surname Analysis

Example: GRAY

Variations of the name: Gray, Graye, Grey, de Grey, Greye, MacGray, McGray, McGrah, McGreay, McGrey.

Origins:

(i) Nickname - name for a man with grey hair or beard (from the Old English graeg, or 'grey')

(ii) Location - from the Norman village of Graye in Calvados, France; GRAYs with this origin of the name first came to Britain after the Norman Conquest of 1066.

Resources: Basil Cottle, *Dictionary of Surnames* (Penguin, 1978); John Titford, *Searching for Surnames* (Countryside Books, 2002); www.nationaltrustnames.org.uk

Quiz Answers

Ale Draper: A seller of ale (often in an ale-house).

Ankle Beater: A young person, who helped drive cattle to market.

Clay Puddler: A maker of clay (the kind used on canals & dams). Often he puddled the clay with his feet.

Crofter: Scottish agricultural tenant; ran his own 'croft' (small agricultural area of land).

Cutler: A maker, seller or sharpener of knives.

Felmonger: Preparer of (for tanning) - or dealer in - sheep's hides & fleeces.

Haberdasher: A dealer in household articles (especially hats and gloves)

Knacker: A harness/ saddle maker (16th century) OR a buyer of artefacts from old houses etc.(19th century).

Ostler: A groom or manager of horses at an inn.

Rag & Bone Man: A travelling dealer of old clothes, furnishings etc.

Reeve: A minor local official for a manor or estate (e.g. a bailiff or churchwarden).

Tallow Chandler: A seller or maker of tallow (fat from sheep or cows) candles.

Victualler: A seller of victuals (food or drink); licensed victualler is often an innkeeper or landlord of a pub

Yeoman: A holder of a small landed estate OR a member of a military yeomanry force.

Picture Credits: The illustrations in *Family History for Kids* were drawn by Antony Cummins (www.achmed-art.co.uk). All other imagery was supplied by the Jolly family, except the photograph on page 21, courtesy of the Popey Family Papers.

Acknowledgements: This book would not have been possible without the contributions of: the late Jack and Gertie Billingham; Robin Brierley; Simon, Jacob & Oscar Causer; Jonathan Cohen; Antony Cummins; Penny Fox; Finny Fox-Davies; Paul and Carolyn Hedges; Barry & Alethea Jolly; Charlotte Jolly; the late Doris Jolly; Edward, Owen & Aurora Jolly; Ian and Vonnie Jolly; Owen and Elizabeth Jolly; Lara, and Spencer Jolly; Keith Miller; Jeremy and Jules Phillips; Natasha Raddon; and Lisa Snaith.